THE
BIVOCATIONAL
PASTOR

THE BIVOCATIONAL PASTOR

Two Jobs,
One Ministry

DENNIS BICKERS

Beacon Hill Press of Kansas City
Kansas City, Missouri

Copyright 2004
by Beacon Hill Press of Kansas City

ISBN 083-412-1301

Printed in the
United States of America

Cover Design: Ted Ferguson

Library of Congress Cataloging-in-Publication Data

Bickers, Dennis W., 1948-
    The bivocational pastor : two jobs, one ministry / Dennis Bickers.
       p. cm.
    Includes bibliographical references.
    ISBN 0-8341-2130-1 (pbk.)
    1. Clergy—Secular employment. I. Title.
    BV676.5.B52 2004
    253'.2—dc22

                                                                2004001475

10 9 8 7 6 5 4 3 2 1

Contents

Acknowledgments

I want to thank several people who made this book possible. I appreciate the people at Beacon Hill Press who believed in this book. Their interest in this book and in bivocational ministry has been a great blessing to me.

My wife, Faye, has been a source of encouragement to me throughout our marriage. She has often believed in me more than I believed in myself. Thank you for allowing me to spend the time it took to write this book, and thank you for all your support over the years. I do love you.

I also want to thank my parents, Clyde and Phyllis Bickers. The values they instilled in me during my childhood years continue to shape my life. Mom went to be with the Lord a few years ago, but the values they taught me live on and are found throughout this book. I am privileged to be their son. Dad and Mom, I dedicate this book to you.

Introduction

I remember reading about a pastor who was attending a denominational meeting and overheard some people talking about a pastor who had left a very "significant" ministry to accept another place of service. For days that statement haunted him. He wondered if anyone considered his current ministry a "significant" one. Did *he* consider it to be a "significant" ministry, or was he simply preparing himself for the next rung on the pastoral ladder? How could he, or anyone, measure significance or success in the ministry?

For 20 years I served as the bivocational pastor of a small rural church in Indiana. During those two decades of ministry these were questions I asked myself many times. I recently resigned from that church to begin work as an area minister with the American Baptist Churches of Indiana and Kentucky. As I work with the pastors of smaller churches, I hear them asking the same questions. Every pastor who believes he or she has been called by God to serve as a minister desires to make a difference. We want to be used by God to touch the lives of other people in a significant way. At retirement, every pastor wants to look back at his or her years of service and feel a sense of accomplishment. Even more important, when we stand before God, each of us wants to hear Him say, "Well done, good and faithful servant. . . . Enter into the joy of your Lord" (Matt. 25:23).

But how do we measure success in a bivocational ministry? After my first book, *The Tentmaking Pastor: The Joy of Bivocational Ministry*, was released, a "fully funded" pastor friend asked if the title wasn't an oxymoron. He asked, "How can you find joy in bivocational ministry? I don't see how you guys do it." Some might wonder if "success in bivocational ministry" isn't another oxymoron. However, I firmly believe that one can enjoy tremendous success in bivocational ministry. This book is written to help you do this.

In chapter 1 we will define success in bivocational ministry. If we don't know what success is, we won't be able to plan for it, and we won't recognize it when we do achieve it. Chapters 2 through 11 will discuss various qualities that make for successful ministry. Please don't get upset if you find you're weak in some of these qualities. Each of these can be learned, and as we grow in these areas, we enable our ministries to become more successful. Ministry is a lifelong process of growing and maturing. When you finish reading a chapter, take some time for careful evaluation before moving on to the next. There will be some self-evaluation questions at the end of each chapter to help you with that process.

As bivocational ministers, we face unique challenges. Along with our family and church responsibilities, we have a second job that requires a certain amount of our time each week. The churches we lead are often smaller churches with few resources. Many of them have plateaued or are in decline. A large number of us serve with little or no formal theological training. Bivocational ministry is looked at by some as "second-class" ministry performed by people who don't have the gifts to serve a larger church. At times, those who don't understand the need for bivocational ministers question our commitment to ministry. Some continue to refer to us as "part-time" preachers.

Each of these challenges can threaten our self-esteem and cause us to question the value of the ministry we provide. My bivocational friend, let me remind you that we follow in the tradition of the apostle Paul, who made tents while he spread the gospel to the world. For much of Christian history, bivocational ministers led the churches. It was not until the 20th century that we found churches moving toward having "fully funded" pastors rather than bivocational pastors.[1]

However, we're already seeing that trend begin to reverse itself in at least one large denomination. Southern Baptists are predicting that within 10 years bivocational pastors will outnumber "fully funded" pastors in their denomination.[2] God is calling more people into bivocational ministry because of the gifts and experiences they can bring to their churches. If God believes we can be successful in our calling, it's time we also begin to believe we can have a successful ministry.

I do have one concern about writing this book. Please don't think I have climbed the mountain of success and am giving you directions to follow so you can join me. I consider myself to be on a success journey with you.

1 Defining Success

As the owner of a heating and air-conditioning company, I receive at least one invitation each week to attend a seminar that will teach me how to grow my company. For the past few years, consolidators have been buying smaller companies and rolling them into larger ones. Utility companies have also entered the heating and air-conditioning business. Small companies such as mine often struggle to compete with these large competitors. Many have decided to close shop.

As the pastor of a church, I receive numerous invitations to attend conferences that will teach me how to grow my church. Recently I received a magazine for Christian leaders that had advertisements for 10 such conferences in it. Pastors often lead these conferences, teaching others the principles they used to grow their churches. They assure us that we will never grow our churches without "seeker-sensitive" services, video projectors, target audiences, cell groups, multiple worship services, and praise teams. They warn that people will abandon us in favor of the growing megachurches, which will offer all these things and even more to their congregations.

It's no wonder that many bivocational pastors in their smaller churches are discouraged. Both worlds in which they live send the same message—bigger is better, and success is often determined by size. They see the wonderful things God is doing in other churches and wonder what went wrong in their own ministries.

Unfortunately, too many of us have accepted some common myths about successful ministries:

- To be successful, my ministry must be big.
- To be significant, my ministry must be in a big place.
- One measure of the significance of my ministry is how much recognition I receive for it.
- Career advances are signs of a significant ministry.[1]

If these are the measures of success, most bivocational ministers will never be considered successful. Too many of us believe we are inadequate and are failing in the ministry because we measure ourselves by the above standards. The problem is that we have allowed other people to establish faulty standards by which we judge our success or failure. Steve Bierly is correct when he writes, "The Lord doesn't want our identity and self-worth as pastors to be bound up in results."[2] We need to determine true, biblical standards of successful ministry and compare ourselves to those standards.

Definitions of Success

Robert Schuller defines success as "discovering and developing your potential as well as seeing the new opportunities born all around you every new day!"[3] John Maxwell's definition of success is "knowing God and his desires for me; growing to my maximum potential; and sowing seeds that benefit others."[4] Charles Stanley writes, "Success is the continuing achievement of becoming the person God wants you to be and accomplishing the goals God has helped you set."[5] Edward Dayton asks,

> How, then, should we define success? The first question of the Westminster Shorter Catechism asks, "What is the chief end of man?" The answer given is "The chief end of man is to give glory to God and enjoy him forever." That defines our primary purpose in life and shows us where we find success.[6]

Notice that none of these definitions of success say anything about the size of our churches, recognition by our peers, or career advancements. They do speak of our relationship to God and our responsibility to develop the potential God has placed within us. Let's take a brief look at each of these and see how they relate to success.

Our Relationship with God

In Josh. 1 we find Joshua preparing to lead the Israelites into the Promised Land. God promises to be with him as He was with Moses and assures him that he will prosper if he will observe the laws of God (v. 7). God then gives Joshua, and us, the secret of genuine success: "This Book of the Law shall not depart from your mouth, but you shall meditate in it day and night, that you may observe to do according to all that is written in it. For then you will make your way prosperous, and then you will have good *success*" (v. 8, italics added).

God called us to be something before He called us to do something. As recipients of the grace of God, we're to grow and develop as Christians. Leith Anderson is correct when he writes, "The call of a Christian is first and foremost to be a follower of Jesus Christ. Any call to leadership or to a specific type of place of ministry is secondary at best. Our call is to be what Jesus wants us to be and to do what Jesus wants us to do."[7]

Joshua's success as a leader was dependent upon his relationship with God. As he and the Israelites followed the laws of God, they enjoyed success. Disobedience to God resulted in failure and tragedy.

True success for the Christian, whether a pastor or layperson, is found in applying God's Word to his or her life. I have a Christian friend who owns a small business. He and a customer, who is also a Christian, disagreed over a bill the business owner sent his client. It appeared the bill would not be paid. The business owner's employees believed the matter should be settled in court, but the owner refused. He believed, based upon 1 Cor. 6:1-8, that it was better for him to take the loss than to sue a fellow Christian. It was more important for my friend to obey the teachings of scripture than to receive the disputed money. Obedience to God sometimes carries a price but will always lead to personal spiritual growth. That growth leads to true success in life.

Developing to Our Potential

"The only true measure of success is the ratio between what we might have been and what we have become. In other words, success comes as the result of growing to our potential."[8]

In Matt. 25 Jesus tells a parable of a man preparing to take a long trip. He called his servants and divided his money between them according to their abilities. One servant was entrusted with five talents; one received two talents, while the third servant was given only one talent. When the man returned from his trip, he asked for an accounting from his servants. The first two servants were able to return to the master twice the talents given to them. Each of them received the same commendation from the master: "Well done, good and faithful servant; you were faithful over a few things, I will make you ruler over many things. Enter into the joy of your lord" (vv. 21, 23). However, the third servant had buried his one talent, and that was all he was able to return to his master. That servant was rebuked and cast out of the presence of the master. Why? Because this servant refused to use the talent he had been given.

Recently I attended a pastor's prayer luncheon in the largest church in our area. The choir loft in the church seats three times what the sanctuary of my church, Hebron, holds. Sixteen thousand people attend services in this church every weekend.

It would have been so easy to leave this church feeling intimidated and questioning my value to the kingdom of God, but I didn't. I left there amazed at what God was doing through the life of that pastor and his staff. He and I have different gifts and a different calling on our lives. Frankly, I don't believe I would have the organizational gifts to lead that church. God called that pastor to lead a very large church in his city. God called me to lead a small bivocational church in our community. Each calling is equally valid and important.

On Judgment Day God won't compare me to this other pastor. He won't compare you to another minister. He won't question why we didn't use gifts He had not given us. He *will* question how each of us used the ones He *did* give us. In other words, did we live up to our potential? If we grew and developed to our potential, we, too, will hear the words of the Lord, "Well done, good and faithful servant." At that time we'll know we achieved true success.

Seeking Success

Is it right for a minister to seek success? There are some who would argue that we are called only to be faithful. Certainly there are times when success is simply remaining faithful to the ministry and vision God has given us despite any outward signs that our ministry is having a significant impact on the lives of people.

During my pastorate at Hebron we enjoyed seasons of God's blessings on our ministry, but we also saw times when God seemed to be doing little in our church. These dry times often tempt the pastor to give up, dust off the résumé, and begin looking for another church. Personally, I believe that pastors who do that often miss out on tremendous blessings that are about to be enjoyed. Dry times may be times of preparation as God is getting us ready for His next move in our lives. Moses spent 40 years in Midian while God was preparing him to lead the Israelites out of Egypt. Joseph spent years as a slave in Egypt, often mistreated and forgotten, before God elevated him to a position where he could save the world from the coming famine. After his Damascus road experience, the apostle Paul spent three years in Arabia and Damascus (Gal. 1:17-18) before beginning his incredible ministry.

As important as faithfulness is, it's not unchristian to seek success in ministry. Leith Anderson encourages us to "seek success. . . . there is nothing proud or inappropriate in determining what success should look like and how to achieve it.[9] As a minister, you want your life and ministry to count. You want your ministry to touch the lives of people in a significant way. In other words, you want to enjoy a successful and fruitful ministry. Develop a vision of what success in your ministry will look like, and then determine how you can best achieve it. If you refuse to do that, it's unlikely you'll experience the success you would like.

That, I believe, is poor stewardship of the gifts and responsibilities God gave us.

The Success Journey

For Charles Stanley, "Success is an *ongoing pursuit.* . . . No person ever truly achieves success."[10] Similarly, to John Maxwell, "Success is a journey rather than a destination."[11] Both of these men certainly have known success. Each has grown large churches, written numerous books, and is in great demand for speaking engagements. By every definition of the word, they are successful Christian leaders. Yet their comments above reveal that neither believes he has achieved success. Their lives and ministries model for us the truth that success is not something to be achieved but a process to be lived.

The life and ministry of the apostle Paul teaches us the same truth. In Phil. 3:12-14 he wrote,

> Not that I have already attained, or am already perfected; but I press on, that I may lay hold of that for which Christ Jesus has also laid hold of me. Brethren, I do not count myself to have apprehended; but one thing I do, forgetting those things which are behind and reaching forward to those things which are ahead, I press toward the goal for the prize of the upward call of God in Christ Jesus.

What does the success journey look like? It starts when you decide you want to succeed in what you do.[12] I see too many ministers who merely seek to survive. They are quick to discuss the difficulties of their ministries—the long hours, the conflicts that exist in their churches, time spent away from families, and the other problems associated with ministry. While they sincerely believe they have been called to the ministry, too often they fall into a survival mode instead of seeking to be successful in the ministry God has given them. We need to determine that we want to be successful in our ministries.

Rick Pitino has been a successful basketball coach at Providence College, the University of Kentucky, and at the professional level. One of the reasons for his success is that he teaches his teams that if they want to be winners, they must deserve to win:

> You want to succeed? Okay, then succeed. Deserve it. How? Outwork everybody in sight. Sweat the small stuff. Sweat the big stuff. Go the extra mile. But whatever it takes, put your heart and soul into everything you do. Leave it all out on the court. . . . Success is not a lucky break. It is not a divine right. It is not an accident of birth. Success is a choice.[13]

We need to make the same type of commitment to our ministries. Anyone who thinks ministry is easy should never become a minister. It is hard, challenging work that demands our best effort. Successful ministry requires even more of us. This is especially true of bivocational ministry, in which there are opportunities to grow in faith, visionary leadership, relationship building, dedication, and passion or to settle for mere survival and risk succumbing to discouragement, low self-esteem, and halfhearted devotion. How we choose to approach our ministry is up to us. We will probably not enjoy a successful ministry unless we decide to move out of the survival mode and pursue success.

The remaining chapters of this book will examine different qualities you must have in your life and ministry if you want to be successful in bivocational ministry. Each of these can be learned and developed, but remember that this is a lifelong pursuit of success. Don't try to shortchange the process, and please don't take a detour around any of these qualities. A person who violates his or her integrity for a short-term goal will not enjoy long-lasting success. Rather, he or she should seek long-term success that will come as "the result of the small victories we accumulate every day."[14] Commit yourself to applying these qualities to your life daily.

I enjoy hearing Zig Ziglar speak at seminars. He begins his lectures by asking two questions:

1. How many of you believe that regardless of how bad your personal, family, and business lives are at this moment there are still some things you could do that would make them even worse?

2. How many of you believe that regardless of how good your personal, family, and business lives are, there are still some things you could do to improve them?[15]

Ziglar asks these questions to help people understand that they need to take responsibility for their futures. Regardless of how successful your ministry is today, it can be even better. If you are currently struggling in your ministry, you can take hope that it can improve. But you have to make it happen. You have to decide that you want a successful ministry that will make a significant impact on the lives of those God has given you to lead. If you've made that decision, then let's begin our success journey.

Reflections

- What is your definition of success?
- Do you consider your present ministry to be successful?
- Since beginning your ministry, do you believe you have grown in your relationship with God, or has that relationship been harmed because of the demands of ministry?
- Do you see success as a journey or a destination?
- Do you believe you should seek success in your ministry?

2　A Good Match

When I yielded to God's call on my life to preach, I had the opportunity to preach in various churches before being asked to serve as an interim pastor for a church in which I was raised. I spent five months in that church before they called a new pastor. By then I knew that God called me to be a pastor, but I was unsure what to do about it. A few weeks later, I heard of a small church that had been without a pastor for over a year. I sent a résumé directly to the church. I informed them that I had no ministerial training or experience but that I believed that God had called me to the ministry, and I was interested in talking to them about their pastoral position.

(Now before I go further, I'm aware that other churches have different procedures for calling a pastor. Some use their local governing boards; others use search committees. There are other differences as well, but the principles I will be sharing work in any denominational setting. So throughout this book make whatever adjustments you feel are needed to adapt these principles to your church's polity.)

Several weeks passed, and then I heard from the church. An interview was set up with their search committee. Looking back, I realize that neither the committee nor I asked the questions we should have asked of one another. Still, they recommended me to the church, and I became their pastor by a unanimous vote. I served as the pastor of that church for 20 years.

The church and I were both fortunate. Neither of us truly knew the other. The church asked me nothing about my theology or ministry philosophy. That was probably good, because I didn't have much philosophy at that time! I did not know much of the church's history, the direction in which it wanted to move, or anything else about the church.

In the past 20 years many churches have contacted me asking if I might be interested in a pastoral change. I met with less than a handful of these churches and developed a list of questions to ask them. Later in this chapter I'll list these questions, but first let's take a look at why it is so important for the minister and church to know one another as well as possible.

Because most bivocational churches are heavily dependent upon relationships, it's important that there be a good match between pastor and church. A church that places great importance upon pastoral care of its members will have problems with a pastor who believes that his or her primary ministry is evangelism. A very traditional pastor may find it difficult to work in a church that wants to be "seeker-sensitive" and on the cutting edge of ministry. In neither of these examples is the church or the pastor wrong; they just have different expectations of ministry. It's highly unlikely that the churches or the pastors in these examples will enjoy a successful ministry.

A marriage relationship is more likely to be healthy and mutually rewarding for the husband and wife who took the time to truly get acquainted with one another before they married. The same is true for the relationship between the minister and church. The difficulty is that there are not usually several months of dating and engagement for the minister and church.

The decision to call a minister is often made after a few contacts and hearing the candidate preach a trial sermon. Many smaller churches are often uncomfortable without a pastor and will try to quickly fill the position without really determining the qualities and gifts their next pastor should have. The bivocational minister may be tempted to accept the church's call due to a fear that other churches will not be interested in a minister who is bivocational. When two strangers enter into such a relationship, we should not be surprised when problems soon erupt.

Churches and their pastoral candidates must take time to learn about one another. Churches usually ask for references from the candidate. Ministers should also check references on the churches that are interviewing them. Contact denominational officials if the church belongs to a denomination. Call other ministers in the area. Find out if the church has a reputation of being difficult to lead or if it has recently had a major conflict. If the church is nondenominational, ask about its theology and doctrine to see if it would be similar to yours. If the facility is close enough to your community, take an afternoon drive to see what it looks like.

This will sound unspiritual to some people, and they won't want to do these things. In my opinion, it's a lot more unspiritual to accept the pastorate of a church and then find out you're in a church that's not a good fit. I have seen pastors spend years trying to lead their churches and meeting resistance with every step they took. Watching them was like watching a person try to push a rope. Some finally realized their churches had different ideas about ministry than they had, and they moved on to other places of service. Others became so frustrated that they left the ministry. A lot of wasted time and effort could have been avoided if the church and the minister had spent more time learning about each other beforehand.

After learning as much as you can about the church, you may decide to proceed with further discussions with the search committee. You need to be prepared for this meeting with a series of questions that will help you better understand this church. I always tell the committee that I will have questions for them when we meet.

I allow the search committee to ask me their questions first. The discussion that follows often answers many of my questions without my having to ask them. Incidentally, I have my questions typed out on two pieces of paper, and I write down the answers I receive for later review. There's a lot going on during these meetings, and I don't want to have to depend on my memory for the answers afterward.

Two things frequently happen when I begin to ask my questions. One is that everyone quickly realizes that I'm asking many more questions than the committee did. While I've never had a committee become upset at my questions, many of them have commented that I asked many more questions than did anyone else they had ever interviewed.

The second thing that often happens is that the committee is uncertain as to how to answer some of the questions, because these are questions the church has not discussed. Even if you don't become their pastor, you may help them become a stronger church, because your questions will make them think.

The questions I ask pastoral search committees have come from a number of sources. Many of them came from Douglas Scott,[1] while others originated elsewhere. I've added a few on my own because I felt they're important.

The Questions

- Why am I of particular interest to you?
- What has been the most significant event in the life of this church since you have been a member?
- Besides looking for a pastor, what has been the most upsetting event in the life of this church?
- In your opinion, what areas of concern need to be addressed by this church?
- What kinds of things did your former pastor do particularly well?
- What were the circumstances surrounding your former pastor's departure?
- In what areas do you wish your former pastors had more expertise?
- In the past, how have you helped your pastors be better ministers? Do you provide time and funds for continuing education?

- Tell me about the boards.
  How are they elected?
  How often are elections held?
  Is there rotating membership on boards?
- Who's in charge of
  Stewardship?
  Christian Education?
  Youth?
  Missions?
  Building maintenance?
- Who's responsible for church-staff relations?
- Has the pastor's family traditionally taken an active role in this church?
- How is the pastor's compensation package determined?
- How frequently is it reviewed?
- Who reviews it?
- What factors are considered in determining the package?
- Are there merit or cost-of-living increases?
- Is there Social Security reimbursement?
- Is there reimbursement for continuing education, books, automobile expenses?
- How should your pastor spend his or her time?
  How much time in prayer?
  How much time in personal study?
  How much time in sermon preparation?
  How much time in administration?
  How much time in counseling?
  How much time for visitation?
  How much time for family?
- What organizations in the church are the most active?
- Besides calling a pastor, and its related concerns, what is the highest congregational priority for the next year?
- What goals have been established for church growth?
- What methods can be used to achieve those goals?

- Are there any plans to expand the staff or the facility?
- How stable is the church financially?
- Is there any indebtedness?
- Are there problems making the budget?
- What are the future financial needs of the church?
- What do you see for this church in the next 10 years?
- What is the potential for growth?
- From what areas does the church attract most of its members?
- Have there been any changes in the worship format lately? What effect did these changes have on the church?
- Are relationships with other area churches friendly?
- What are the feelings of the church toward the denomination?
- Have there been any theological or practical divisions in the church in the past five years?
- How are people received into membership in this church?
- Are people of all races and cultures welcome to attend and become members of this church?

It will take some time to receive answers to all these questions; that's why I tell the search committee about them beforehand. In some situations, we had to schedule additional meetings to give the committee time to respond.

Although it's time consuming and at times a little embarrassing to ask some of these questions, it's essential that you know as much about the church as you can prior to making any decision. It's much better to take the time now than to deal with the problems that would come if you were not a good match for the church.

A number of years ago I interviewed with a church that wanted to consider me for their pastorate. The interview was going very well, and it appeared that we might be a good match. One of the committee members even stated that he saw no need to interview anyone else. However, I still had a couple of questions left.

I asked the final question on my list: "Are people of all races and cultures welcome to attend and become members of this church?" The committee members assured me that everyone was welcome to attend their church and that minorities had attended there in the past. I explained that I asked that question because my daughter is married to an African-American, and I wanted to make sure they would be welcome to worship there when they came home to visit. The atmosphere in the room changed immediately, and everyone's discomfort was obvious. Within minutes the interview ended, and I never heard from that church again.

What if I had not asked that question? I might have gone to that church not really knowing their attitudes about people of other races. We would have found ourselves in an awkward situation, and my time there would probably have been very short.

Take the time to ask your questions. It's essential to the success of your ministry and the church's that there be a good fit between you.

Reflections

- How do you prepare for an interview with a church that's considering you for their pastorate?
- What things about a church would you want to know about before accepting their call to become their pastor? Make a list, and prepare some questions that will help you learn these things.

3 Vision for the Church

Moses is an excellent example of a leader with a vision. God called Moses to lead the Israelites out of Egyptian slavery to a new land He had promised to Abraham and his descendants. During the Exodus the Israelites continually focused on the problems they encountered. Moses, on the other hand, concentrated on the vision God had given him. Moses saw the problems as merely obstacles to overcome while he fulfilled the vision God gave him. His task was to lead the Israelites to the place God wanted them. He successfully completed that task only because he stayed focused on his God-given vision.

What Is Vision?

George Barna defines vision as "a clear mental portrait of a preferable future, communicated by God to His chosen servant-leaders, based upon an accurate understanding of God, self, and circumstances."[1] Robert Dale reminds us: "A legitimate Christian vision isn't just positive thinking or fuzzy guesses; real vision grows out of Jesus' kingdom dream and steers us into profound and practical ministries."[2] Vision will also entail risk. Andy Stanley states that "just about every God-ordained vision appears to be impossible."[3] If there is no risk associated with the vision, it's likely that someone merely has a good idea.[4] A true vision will be so large and challenging that the power of God is required to fulfill it.

A pastor with a vision for his or her church understands what God wants to do in and through that church. He or she has a much broader view than anyone else. While the Christian education board focuses on the church's educational tasks, the treasurer on the church's finances, and the trustees on the church's physical property, the visionary pastor understands how all these elements must work together to achieve the plans God has for the church.

Visionaries Are Not Just Dreamers

As an area minister, I often work with churches that are looking for a new pastor. I usually begin my meeting with them by asking what they believe God's vision is for their church. Few churches can answer that question. Virtually every church responds with answers that don't so much reflect God's vision as they do the church's own desire for survival. Most respond that they need to reach young families or that they need to revive their once flourishing youth program. However, no one has any idea of how to achieve this. The smaller churches especially are waiting for a pastor to come who can help them achieve these dreams.

Unfortunately, many pastors are also more dreamers than visionaries. They often understand the needs of their churches but have no idea as to how to achieve them. They pray asking God to send young families or youth to their churches. They challenge their congregations to pray that God would do a great work in their churches. Prayer is important—vital—but we must be sure we're praying for the right thing. While it's true that we can do nothing without God, God's plan has always been to work through people who want to make a difference. Dreamers are content to wish things were different; visionaries seek ways to partner with God to make a difference. Andy Stanley points out that Nehemiah was a true visionary and not just a dreamer:

It is interesting that Nehemiah never prayed for God to rebuild the wall. What he prays for is an *opportunity* to go rebuild it himself. That is the difference between a dreamer and a visionary. Dreamers dream about things being different. Visionaries envision themselves making a difference. Dreamers think about how nice it would be for something to be done. Visionaries look for an opportunity to do something.[5]

Dreaming is killing our churches. The reason many of our churches simply dream of better things is that they have been led by dreamers and not visionaries. All a congregation knows is that things should be different, so they ask God to do something in their church, and they continually seek a pastor who will lead them in fulfilling their dreams. While this is a problem in many churches, it seems most prevalent in the smaller church.

As bivocational ministers model true visionary leadership, their churches will not only be transformed but also understand the difference between dreaming and truly seeking God's vision. Understanding this difference can lead to a church's enjoying a long-term successful ministry.

How Important Is Vision?

Prov. 29:18 states, "Where there is no vision, the people perish" (KJV). Many churches struggle today because no one has caught God's vision. Vision provides direction and purpose. A lack of vision often results in chaos. Rather than providing leadership to his or her church, the pastor without a vision often spends time coping with problems and conflicts. Too many pastors can identify with the one who said, "I have pastored congregations in Oklahoma and Pennsylvania and refereed two churches in Ohio!"[6]

Smaller churches frequently operate without a clear vision. As a result, many struggle to survive, and every week some lose the battle and lock their doors. About four thousand churches in America die every year.[7] What a tragedy! While some churches are shutting down, many denominations are starting new churches as a way of reaching new people for Christ. These new church plants are often successful in the same areas where the other churches failed. This is often because the new churches have a vision of what God wants to do through them, while the established churches did not.

One major reason these smaller churches often lack a vision is that they experience a high pastoral turnover. It's not uncommon for small churches in our area to have new pastoral leadership every 12 to 18 months. The pastors are often seminary students who seek new churches after they graduate. These "student pastorates" enable seminarians to get some practical experience while pursuing their theological education, but the churches themselves often suffer due to a lack of genuine pastoral leadership and vision.

One of the advantages of bivocational ministry is that a minister can remain in the smaller church longer. The longer pastorate allows trust to build between the church and the pastor, and building trust is an essential element of a successful ministry.[8] Remaining at the same church for a longer time also allows the pastor to better understand the community in which the church ministers. Vision is often just understanding the needs of the area and the church and how God would have you respond to those needs.

I once heard a minister say, "The need is the call." He was complaining about Christians who claim they would minister if they only felt called to some ministry. He challenged believers to look around for existing needs and understand that they are called to minister to those needs. I believe the same is true for the church. As we spend longer periods of time serving our church and community, we will better understand the ministry needs that exist. Vision will spring out of that understanding.

Searching for their next pastor is the only vision too many of our smaller churches ever have. That's one reason I'm so excited that bivocational ministry is growing in acceptance today. A bivocational minister can remain in his or her church for extended periods of time, develop a vision for the church, and lead it to achieve that vision.

Many existing churches have not experienced any significant growth in years. A lack of vision has robbed them of the vitality and purpose they once enjoyed. These churches may exist for decades, but they accomplish virtually nothing for the kingdom of God. Rick Warren has some advice for the pastors of such churches:

If you serve in an existing church that has plateaued, is declining, or is simply discouraged, your most important task is to *redefine* your purpose. . . . Recapture a clear vision of what God wants to do in and through your church family. Absolutely nothing will revitalize a discouraged church faster than rediscovering its purpose.[9]

Receiving the Vision

How does a pastor receive God's vision for his or her church? Sometimes the vision will just come as it did with Moses when he approached the burning bush. Moses was not seeking a new vision or new duties. He was content to provide for his family and flock. But God sought Moses out and revealed to him His plans for the Hebrews. By contrast, for most of us the vision will come when we begin to seek God's purpose for our church. This requires time and much prayer.

The word "time" sends up immediate red flags for most bivocational ministers. We don't have time now to do everything that needs to be done. We spend time preparing sermons, being with our families, visiting the sick, meeting with committees, and working in our second jobs. Where are we going to find time to seek a vision for our churches? I understand these feelings, because I had the same thoughts until recent years.

For much of my ministry I was content to enjoy the occasional successes we enjoyed as a church. However, we were a church that was drifting, because I was a pastor who was drifting. Each year my first sermon was a statement about my vision for the church, but it was so general that it provided us with little direction. Successes can come when you are drifting, but so can problems.

The Ohio River flows alongside our town. Occasionally I'll take my boat to the river to fish for bass. Often I'll pull alongside a stretch of bank and fish that bank while the river's current moves me along. I've never had any troubles on the river when I was running my engine or trolling motor, but I've had many problems while drifting. My engine has been lodged on underwater rocks and jammed between logs, and I've had to stop fishing to get my boat loose. One day the engine caught on a rock, and the boat lurched in the current and nearly threw me overboard. Although I was able to fall into the boat rather than out of it, I fell on six of my fishing rods, breaking all of them and sticking a couple of hooks in my arm. I got into trouble because I was drifting and not moving with a purpose.

Without a vision, the pastor and the church are just drifting, and this will often lead to problems. Seeking a vision is not a waste of time—it's one of the most important things a pastor can do for his or her church. It's unfortunate that many people today don't value thinking, but the pastor must spend time thinking through the vision and the means to achieve it. Some questions to ask during this time include

- Who are we?
- Where do we live?
- What is God calling us to do?[10]

Such questions must be bathed in prayer. In fact, I would encourage you to ask others in your church to pray with you as you seek God's vision for the church. A group in our church meets each Sunday evening before our evening worship service to pray specifically for my wife and me and for our church. Occasionally I ask them to pray for me as I seek God's direction for the church. It's a powerful thing to hear them ask God to reveal what He wants to do in our church and community.

Sharing the Vision

John Maxwell rightly states, "The success of a vision is determined by its ownership by both the leader and the people."[11] A pastor friend of mine told me that he used to announce his vision to the congregation and take their nodding heads as a sign of affirmation. He could not understand why there was seldom any action taken to achieve the vision. He finally learned that their nodding heads merely indicated their agreement that this was something worthwhile for him to pursue! He owned the vision—not them. Thus, it was his responsibility to make it happen. As pastors, we have to ensure that the church and pastor jointly share ownership of the vision.

One advantage that bivocational ministers have is that their churches often understand that they have responsibilities outside the church and are willing to share the load of ministry with them. However, people are too busy to involve themselves in work that lacks direction and purpose. They want to feel their work in the church has value. When they share ownership of a vision for the church, they'll find that value in working to make that vision a reality.

A vision for the church should often first be shared privately with the key people in the church. It's essential that these people buy into the vision before it's shared with the whole church. Smaller churches are often not excited about changes, and without the support of the key people in the congregation, the church may refuse to buy into the vision if it will entail much change.

As the pastor, you must determine who the key people are to make this vision a reality. It may or may not be everyone on your board. In fact, it may be a matriarch or patriarch in the church who doesn't even hold an official leadership position. Those who will exert the most influence over the acceptance or rejection of the vision are the ones you need to contact first. Their support will go a long way toward gaining the support of rest of the church.

What do you do if they refuse to support the vision? I believe George Barna is right when he says, "Vision . . . is not determined by a two-thirds vote; it is not the result of consensus of interested parties; and vision is not identified through a committee-based process."[12] However, I also believe that pastors can miss God's leadership. Trying to force a vision upon a church that's not ready to receive it can shorten a pastor's ministry in that church. It may be that the church does not have the resources to move in a particular direction, and the key leaders understand that better than the pastor. Analyze the reasons for the rejection. If they seem to be sound, go back to your prayer closet and continue to seek God's direction. If the reasons appear to be a lack of faith or commitment, then find ways to help them grow in these areas.

If the key leaders support the vision, it's time to present it to the church. It's important to share not only the vision but also how the vision can be accomplished. Do your homework. Be as specific as you can. Demonstrate how achieving this vision is a part of God's plan for the church. "Adding value" is a popular term these days, so tell the church how this vision will add value to their individual lives as well as to the church. Encourage your key leaders to voice their approval of this vision.

Once the congregation owns the vision, it's important to continually keep the vision before the people. Rick Warren suggests, "Vision and purpose must be restated every 26 days to keep the church moving in the right direction."[13] There are many ways to promote the vision. You can use sermons, bulletins, newsletters, programs, and individual meetings with members of the congregation. Be creative, but keep the vision before the people.

Example of a Vision

Two years ago I attended a leadership seminar led by John Maxwell. I left that seminar as I did many before it. I was excited about what I had learned; I knew this was information we needed in our church, but I was uncertain as to how to present it. Maxwell shared in that conference that he had led his first church to grow but had not developed leadership in that church. Consequently, shortly after he left to take another pastorate, much of that growth was lost. Like many pastors, I could identify with that, and I did not want that to happen to my church. Although we had people who were growing in leadership abilities, we needed a good program to develop leadership and to increase our lay ministry.

Maxwell announced he would be returning to the area in about two months to lead a lay ministry conference. When I returned to the church, I began talking about how helpful the seminar had been and that I was excited that he would soon return to lead a similar one. I encouraged our church to attend this second conference, and 10 people signed up. Those who attended became excited about what they were hearing, and we agreed to purchase some material to take back to the church for further training. This material was fairly expensive for our small church, but we made the investment because we saw value in it.

I began sharing with key people the vision I had to help our church develop better leadership skills and become more involved in lay ministry. They responded very well to that, because most of them had attended the lay ministry conference. I studied the material we purchased and found it to be very thorough. Maxwell suggested a format to follow in presenting the material, and I decided to present it accordingly.

On the first Sunday of that year I preached my vision sermon. In the sermon I shared how many of us had attended the conference and believed strongly in the material that was presented. I shared my belief that God wanted us to spend a great deal of time that year in leadership development and lay ministry training. I mapped out the direction this would take. The initial sermons would be delivered on Sunday mornings. We had not had a midweek service for many years, but we would also do leadership training on Wednesday nights for those interested in becoming better leaders in the church, their homes, and their occupations. There would be a Saturday presentation on lay ministry. Following that program, I would begin a series of sermons about spiritual gifts. At the conclusion of that series we would hand out a spiritual gifts assessment. I intended to review with the participants what spiritual gifts this assessment indicated they have. Part of the material would be presented on Sunday nights. In all, we planned to spend the first six months of that year in leadership development and lay ministry training.

The response was great. Almost a fourth of our congregation was involved in this training. They shared the vision that God wanted to train and equip us for even greater service in the future. We believed our church would benefit from this, and we believed we as individuals would grow spiritually as we ministered in the areas in which we were gifted. This vision gave us direction and purpose as a church.

The Bivocational Pastor's Advantage of Having a Vision

Although determining God's vision may seem time-consuming, such vision will actually enable you to minister more effectively. The year we did our leadership training, I knew many of my sermons themes would be about leadership and lay ministry. Time previously spent in the development of sermon themes could then be spent in the preparation of sermons. That saved me much time.

Programming for the year is also simplified. Any program that does not add value to the vision is not considered. As mentioned earlier, we used some of John Maxwell's material for our leadership development and lay ministry training. This material required very little preparation for me to present to the church. We were able to do high-quality training in our church with little extra work on my part. With the wide variety of excellent programs that are available today, you can probably find some that will help you promote the vision you and your church have for your ministry. Use these resources, but you must have a vision for your church before you'll know what resources and programs you'll need.

Perhaps the greatest advantage a vision will bring is that it will help focus your church on its real purpose for existing. Tradition and history guide many bivocational churches more than vision. Many are in a survival mode. As they struggle to keep their doors open, they yearn for the way the church used to be. They believe their best years are behind them.

One of the most difficult tasks the bivocational pastor will have in such churches is to convince them that God wants to do even greater things in their future than He did in their past. But they can't continue to do ministry as it was done in the 1950s. We live in a new culture with different needs and expectations. While we dare not change the message we proclaim to the world, we must change the methods by which we proclaim it.

Too many churches are answering questions no one is asking. They continue to offer programs that don't interest people and wonder why no one responds. In an age of computers and videos, we offer the flannelgraph and wonder why the world considers the church to be irrelevant and out of touch with today's society. I appreciate Rick Warren's comment in this area: "We invite the unchurched to come and sit on seventeenth-century chairs (which we call pews), sing eighteenth-century songs (which we call hymns), and listen to a nineteenth-century instrument (a pipe organ), and then we wonder why they think we're out-of-date!" [14]

Instilling a fresh vision of what God wants to do in the church will help turn around that backward thinking and enable the church to focus on the ministry God seeks to do in the present and in the future. It will fill the congregation with hope and help them dare to dream that perhaps God still does have a purpose for their church. Accomplishing this task may be the most important thing you can do to enjoy a successful bivocational ministry.

Achieving the Vision

Once you have received the vision and the church has accepted ownership of it, the difficult task of achieving it now must be planned. Goal setting is the only way of doing this. Some ministers don't believe in goal setting because they believe it's somehow unspiritual. Others don't set goals because to do it properly takes time. Neither is a good reason—especially since most studies show that people who set goals and work to achieve them are more successful than those who do not. [15]

Goals are simply the stepping-stones that will take you from where you are to where you want to be. Vision shows you where you want to be, and goals help you get there. A vision may be so large that it seems impossible to reach; goals help break that down into smaller pieces. As you fulfill each piece, you come closer to achieving your vision.

Perhaps your church's vision is to increase the membership of the church by 10 percent by the end of the year. One of your goals might be to see 12 people join the church. Another goal may be to offer a nursery during each of the services to attract young families. While there may be many goals, each of them will help fulfill the vision of the church. Rather than looking at the vision and wondering how you'll ever increase the membership of the church by 10 percent, the goals break that down into more manageable pieces.

In order for a goal to actually be a goal, it must contain certain qualities. An acronym I have found to be helpful is that a goal must be a "smart" goal:

S – Specific
M – Measurable
A – Attainable
R – Realistic
T – Time-defined

A goal of seeing your church grow is not really a goal—it's only a dream or a hope. A goal would be stated something like "I want to see my church add 12 new members by December 31 of this year." And this is a smart goal because it meets all the characteristics listed above.

One other quality of a goal is that it must be written on paper. If it's something you carry only in your head, it may be a good idea, but it's not really something to which you're committed.

For the past few years I have been very committed to a program of goals. I use one taught by Zig Ziglar, but there are other good ones available. At the beginning of each year I set certain goals for my family, my ministry, my business, and my own personal development. Every week I determine four goals that I'll focus on that week, and every day I chart my progress on each of them. It takes only a few minutes to examine my activities for the day, but it's time well spent. Success and failure don't just happen to a person; they're the results of daily activities.

The Fear of Failure

One reason many pastors don't cast a vision for their churches or have a program of goals for their lives is the fear of failure. The vision may not be achieved, and the goals may not be realized. If they're persons with low self-esteem, they may be afraid of another failure in their lives. Perhaps they're afraid the church will respond negatively to future plans if this vision does not come to pass. They may be in a situation where previous programs have failed, and they may fear being seen as a poor leader by leading the church in another failing effort.

I would remind such pastors of the apostle Paul's words in 2 Tim. 1:7: "God has not given us a spirit of fear, but of power and of love and of a sound mind." The fears that would hold you back are not from God but from the enemy who would seek to destroy your ministry and the ministry of your church.

The fear of failure ceases to be a problem when you accept that occasional failures will happen. The only people who never fail are those who never attempt new things. Success comes only to those who are willing to risk failure to find new ways of accomplishing great things. A reporter once asked Thomas Edison, "Mr. Edison, how does it feel to have failed 10,000 times in your present venture?" Edison responded, "Young man, I will give you a thought that should benefit you in the future. I have not failed anything 10,000 times. I have successfully found 10,000 ways that will *not* work." Edison actually estimated that he performed over 14,000 experiments before inventing the incandescent light.[16]

Winston Churchill failed at many things in life, yet when his leadership was needed during World War II, he rose to the challenge. His experiences led him to define success as "going from failure to failure without loss of enthusiasm."[17] What a great attitude for a bivocational minister!

I don't achieve every goal I set for myself, but working toward a goal makes me more successful than if I had done nothing. If you set a goal of bringing 20 new people into your church this year and you bring in only 10, you've still experienced growth. If your church has a vision of building a new facility during the next year, but because of financial or zoning reasons you can't achieve that vision, you haven't failed. Your church is working toward a common goal, and this is bringing unity and purpose to the congregation. You may need to address the financial problems and teach the church about stewardship, or look for another location if the zoning issue cannot be resolved. You may want to lead your church in a season of prayer seeking God's direction on the situation. The important thing is that you're still working toward achieving the vision.

Lack of Resources

Another reason bivocational pastors are sometimes reluctant to seek God's vision is the limited resources of their churches. Even if a congregation catches a fresh vision for their church's ministry, the pastor may fear they'll suffer tremendous frustration when they don't have the resources to bring it about.

Many small churches struggle financially, but finances are not the only limited resources in the small church. Time, energy (for churches made up mostly of elderly, retired people), gifts, and abilities are all resources that may be lacking or in short supply.

Erwin Raphael McManus writes, "Our structures are usually adequate for the vision they contain; but when the vision increases, the structures become inadequate."[18] This is one reason we see little change occur in our churches. We have the resources to do what we are doing, but we doubt we would have the resources to do something new. We want to do more in our church, and we may even believe that God is leading us to new things, but the limitations of our resources hold us back.

Henry Blackaby reminds us that "resources should follow vision, not determine it."[19] When God brought visions to the Old Testament prophets, they all had good reasons why they could not fulfill them. God called Moses to lead the Israelites to freedom, and he protested that he could not do this because he was a poor speaker (Exod. 4:10). God provided the speaking resource Moses needed in his brother Aaron. As the Israelites wandered in the desert and needed food and water, God provided it in the form of manna and of water that came from a rock.

Resources are never a problem with God. The problem is that He often does not give us the resources we need until He determines that we're willing to be obedient to the vision He has for us.

When Nehemiah was burdened with the vision to rebuild the wall around Jerusalem, he could have easily refused, thinking he did not have the resources needed to rebuild it. He did not even enjoy the resource of personal freedom. Although he held an important position, he was still a captive in a foreign country. Refusing to focus on his limitations, he focused on God and the vision. He prayed and sought God's direction until the king, noticing his distress, allowed him to make his request to return to Jerusalem to rebuild the wall. Not only did the king approve his request, but he also provided the resources Nehemiah would need to complete the task (Neh. 2:1-8).

I know a church that began to grow after many years of being plateaued. One thing the church wanted was to develop a strong worship service. They had no choir, no one to lead a music program, and no one even to play the piano. They purchased a new piano and believed that God would provide someone to play it. Several months went by before they found a piano player. Today they have a strong praise band, a choir, and a very good worship service. They've also built a new sanctuary and a new family life center and have greatly expanded their parking area. A few years ago this church did not even have a piano player—today it's the fastest-growing church in its community. They refused to allow a lack of resources to keep them from achieving the vision God had given them of a strong worship program.

Vision Is Not an Option

"The only justifiable reason to accept the privilege and responsibility of leadership is to help people accomplish the fruition of a vision from God."[20] This blunt assessment is true for those of us who serve in bivocational ministries. Our churches need more than just another preacher to fill the pulpit until a larger church calls him or her away. They need a fresh vision from God for their future ministry and a rekindled hope that God will again use them to significantly impact the lives of people. For these things they need a leader who will not only cast a vision but also have the courage to lead them in achieving it. Our churches will successfully touch their communities when they begin to minister according to God's vision for them.

Reflections

- What do you believe God's vision is for the church you serve?
- How would your church be different if it ministered according to that vision?
- What goals will you need to reach to achieve this vision?
- Does your church have ownership of this vision? If not, what steps do you need to take for them to share ownership of the vision with you?
- Are you willing to risk failure to accomplish this vision?

4　Leadership in the Church

Bivocational ministers often struggle with providing leadership to their churches. A few patriarchs and matriarchs rather than the pastor have traditionally led the smaller churches we often serve.[1] These churches "are usually connected through family systems. In an established church of fifty or fewer, bloodlines are the glue holding the people together. . . . The pastor can serve the congregation for twenty-five years and still be an outsider because he has no blood relationship in the church."[2]

I'm not suggesting that it will take you 25 years before you can start providing leadership to your church, but it does take time. John Koessler earned the ability to lead his church during his sixth year.[3] Some things happened in my seventh year that let me know that the church was more accepting of my leadership. Leadership is based on trust, and it will take time for a church to begin to trust you enough to allow you to lead it.

What Is Leadership?

George Barna defines leadership as "the sum of the spirit and activity generated by the person who seeks to do the right things at the right times for the right reasons to achieve a specific, predetermined set of outcomes."[4] John Maxwell says, "Leadership is influence."[5] Peter Drucker lists four aspects of leadership:

- The only definition of a *leader* is someone who has *followers*.
- An effective leader is not someone who is loved or admired. . . . Popularity is not leadership. Results are.
- Leaders are highly visible. They therefore set examples.
- Leadership is not rank, privileges, titles, or money. It is responsibility.[6]

All of these definitions are helpful, but one aspect of leadership has not been addressed. The Christian leader is first a servant. One of the lessons Jesus taught His disciples was that leadership was "servantship." In case the disciples did not understand the lesson, Jesus demonstrated it by wrapping a towel around His waist and washing their feet in the Upper Room.

The pastor who wishes to lead must first be willing to serve. "Leadership in the early church was based upon the 'power' to render service and never on 'Lordship,' and one of the chief services which leaders may provide is that of setting an example in loving service."[7]

Some pastors see their role in the church as CEO of the organization. While that model may work in some megachurches, it will not be accepted in the bivocational church. Bivocational churches are looking for a pastor who will love and serve them. Relationships are the important elements in the bivocational church, and the ability to lead will come through those relationships.[8]

Influencing the Influencers

Since it takes several years for the bivocational pastor to earn the trust of the church, how does he or she provide leadership to the church? You lead the church by influencing those in the church who influence others.

A friend of mine accepted the pastorate of a small church. It was his first congregation. People in the community, including some other pastors, told him he would not survive long in that church because of the families who controlled it. He was told that those families would run him out within a year, as they had most previous pastors.

He soon found that these families were leaders in the church and that they were neither evil nor petty. They had a deep love for the Lord and for that little church. He began to develop relationships with them. He sought their counsel when he considered making changes. Their advice was important because the church respected them and often followed their lead. Spending time with these leaders, my friend learned about the history of the church. This helped him better understand the feelings and attitudes of the people. This congregation had experienced pain from previous pastors, and he would have to earn their trust. Because he took time to develop relationships and demonstrated a respect for the church, he eventually earned the right to become one of the leaders. For many years he enjoyed a very successful ministry as their pastor.

My friend would have made a tragic mistake if he had stepped up to the pulpit on his first Sunday and announced that he was now that church's leader. As the pastor he may have had a leadership position, but he was not the leader. The chances are good he would not have survived long enough to have ever been a leader in that church.

Why Is Leadership So Important?

Some bivocational pastors see their ministry as primarily preaching and caring for church members. They spend their time preparing sermons and visiting in the homes and hospital rooms of their members. Certainly, preaching good-quality sermons and providing pastoral care are important, but these are not enough.

Too many of our churches are dead and dying. Long ago they began to decline in numbers and influence. No longer having an impact on their communities, they turned inward and began their struggle to survive. Many were once strong, dynamic churches that were touching their communities for God, but now they are churches in name only. Their passion and spiritual power are gone.

George Barna has studied these churches. While many factors may play a part, he found that the most common reason for a church's decline was that their pastor failed to provide effective leadership.[9]

John Maxwell says, "Everything rises and falls on leadership."[10] This is certainly true of the churches we serve. A church that is spiritually strong and impacting its community has a strong leadership who are casting a vision and leading the church in ministry. A church that is weak and ineffective is merely reflecting its leadership. When a church has experienced weak leadership for a long time, it will have a difficult time recovering.

This is because poor leadership will drive away the leaders you need to accomplish great things for God. George Barna's insights are especially helpful:

> I have discovered that the current exodus from the church is partially attributable to the flight of the laity who possess leadership abilities, gifts, and experience. These individuals, whom the church so desperately needs, are leaving the church because they can no longer stomach being part of an alleged movement that lacks strong, visionary leadership. These are people of capacity, people who can make things happen. I have watched with sorrow as they have tried to penetrate the culture of the church and offer the benefit of their gifts. They have been unable to contribute because their churches are neither led by leaders nor by those who understand leadership.[11]

The Price of Leadership

Although leadership is essential to the success of the ministry, there is a price to be paid for it. One price every leader pays at some time is conflict. Darius Salter reminds us that "inherent in leadership is decision making. Decision making often means conflict, confrontation, pro-con polarization, and sometimes bearing the responsibility of failure."[12]

I personally do not enjoy conflict and try to avoid it whenever possible. However, leaders are going to experience conflict as they make decisions that bring about change in their organizations. Small churches don't like change. People are comfortable with familiar routines. When change is introduced, many people are uncertain as to what their new role will be and become fearful that they won't have a part in the new structure.

When introducing change, it's important to minimize potential conflict. It's always easier to prevent a fire than to put one out. We've already talked about including those who have influence in the church as early as possible. Bruce Powers tells us that "change is accomplished most readily when people who will be affected are involved in the decision-making process."[13]

The leader must be able to explain the advantages the proposed change will mean to the church. People will usually resist change until they believe the advantages of the change outweigh the disadvantages of continuing as they are.[14] A small church was undecided about paving their parking lot. The cost was a concern for the church, and not everyone felt a paved parking lot was worth the expense. Some of the leaders began to explain the benefits a paved parking lot would bring to the church:

- Church growth studies indicated that good parking was important to people searching for a church to attend.
- Snow removal would be easier.
- Less dirt and mud would be tracked onto the church carpet.
- Women wearing high heels would be more comfortable walking on blacktop than on gravel.
- It would improve the appearance of the church property.

The church decided the benefits of the paved parking lot were worth the expense. Within a few months the money was raised to do the work.

Leaders know that sometimes conflict will arise despite every effort to avoid it. The wise leader must determine whether the conflict can be resolved or managed. In a healthy church, conflict does not mean the church cannot move forward. Although some people may disagree with certain decisions, they remain committed to the church's overall vision and are willing to work to see it achieved.

There are also those times of much opposition when it seems as if some within the congregation will do whatever they can to stop the church's progress. In such cases the spiritual leader "will go into immediate action, regardless of consequences. In pursuing his goal, he will have the courage to burn his bridges behind him."[15] Such a leader will be following the example of Nehemiah.

Nehemiah returned to Jerusalem to rebuild the city, the Temple, and the wall that surrounded the city. The monumental task was made more difficult by the opposition he had from some people who did not want to see the protective wall go up. They challenged his authority and threatened to disrupt the construction. His opponents tried to demoralize the workers so they would not complete the work. Nehemiah refused to allow this opposition to keep him from completing the task he believed God had given him. In only 52 days he brought the wall to completion, and this silenced his critics.

There will be times when people will do everything they can to stop your leadership. Some will even resort to lies, gossip, innuendo, and unfair criticism. Stephen Covey has sound advice for the leader experiencing such difficulties:

> Give no answer to contentious arguments or irresponsible accusations. Let such things "fly out open windows" until they spend themselves. If you try to answer or reason back, you merely gratify and ignite pent-up hostility and anger. When you go quietly about your business, the other has to struggle with the natural consequences of irresponsible expression. . . . The power to let arguments fly out open windows flows out of an inward peace that frees you from the compulsive need to answer and justify. The source of this peace is living responsibly, obediently to conscience.[16]

Not every leader will be appreciated by those he or she has been called to lead. The leadership you bring to your congregation may not be recognized until after you leave the church. Remembering the following words has helped me: "Often the crowd does not recognize a leader until he has gone, and then they build a monument for him with the stones they threw at him in life."[17]

Qualifications for a Leader

It was once assumed that a master of divinity degree qualified one to lead a church. Today there is widespread concern that the typical seminary education does not prepare the pastor for the leadership demands he or she will face. Erwin Raphael McManus states the concern well:

> One could almost predict that the development of the Master of Divinity degree would serve as the religious equivalent to the M.B.A. Seminaries began to produce what local churches perceived they needed: godly men who had a professional understanding of theology, pastoral care, and management. Pastors were valued for their ability to bring and keep order rather than their ability to bring and lead change. The reality was that pastors were being equipped to preserve the past rather than create the future. We became known for being traditional rather than transformational. The ritual replaced the radical. The pastor/teacher replaced the apostle/evangelist. . . . Seminaries were producing pastors who were ready for the pulpits but not for the challenge. Pastors found themselves experts in Biblical exegesis, but novices in cultural exegesis.[18]

The smaller church especially has less concern about the academic degrees a pastoral candidate may have and more interest in whether or not he or she can do the job. This is good news for the bivocational minister, because many have no formal education beyond high school.

Please do not misunderstand; I am not opposed to education. While serving as a bivocational pastor, I completed my bachelor's degree and graduated from a Bible school. I recently began working on my master's degree. I know that what I learned in school made me a better minister. But while I believe that education can benefit your ministry, it may not necessarily make you a better leader.

Leith Anderson lists several qualifications he believes the leaders of today's church need. I will list them and briefly talk about some of them. The leader of the 21st-century church needs to

- Understand the culture in which we live
- Be flexible
- Maintain good relations with the members of his [or her] church and community
- Be an entrepreneur
- Be a risk-taker
- Be godly.[19]

One of the criticisms of today's church is that it is not relevant to today's problems and needs. As stated earlier, some churches still minister as if they were living in the 1950s—they answer questions no one is asking anymore and administer programs that are no longer wanted or needed by the people around them. Again, these mistakes occur because they often don't understand the culture in which they live. An effective leader must be able to instill in his or her church a sound grasp of the current issues and concerns affecting the community that surrounds it.

Such a leader must also be flexible. As pastors we often complain about our churches resisting change. The truth is most pastors I know, including myself, are not always comfortable with change either. As the world in which we live changes, we must adapt to those changes, or our ministries will soon become ineffective. Hans Finzel wrote, "In times of change, learners inherit the earth, while the learned find themselves beautifully equipped to deal with a world that no longer exists."[20] Those who remain flexible and continue learning will be the real leaders of the church.

Good relational skills are a must for the pastor who wishes to provide effective leadership. We have already discussed the importance of relationships in the smaller church. If the pastor is seen as cold, distant, or unfriendly, he or she will not last very long as a leader in the bivocational church. The wise pastor will spend time learning about his or her people and relating to them personally and not just professionally.

Maintaining good relations with the community is also important for the pastor who wishes to enjoy a successful ministry in the community. This is an advantage that some bivocational ministers have over "fully funded" ministers. The bivocational minister's second job often places him or her out in the community more. People in the community can see him or her as something else than simply a pastor.

As the owner of a small business, I am involved in the community. We sponsor several activities for the school systems, the parks department, and other organizations. I give a scholarship to a member of the high school baseball team each year. Because we're in a small community, many people know me as both a business owner and a minister. I believe my ministry benefits from my involvement in the community.

The final qualification for a spiritual leader we will discuss is the most important. When the church began looking for people to serve the widows, they looked for men who were full of the Holy Spirit (Acts 6:3). J. Oswald Sanders says being Spirit-filled is the one indispensable qualification for the spiritual leader.[21] Franklin Segler adds:

> Pastoral authority is more an authority of influence than an authority of office. In one sense it grows out of the pastor's character and spiritual discernment and is so recognized by the church. . . . Genuine Christian character and spirituality inspire and encourage followship. As long as a pastor follows Christ, his fellow members are willing to follow him.[22]

Developing Leadership Ability

I remember the first time I heard John Maxwell speak about the "law of the lid," which says that "Leadership ability is the lid that determines a person's level of effectiveness. The lower an individual's ability to lead, the lower the lid on his potential. The higher the leadership, the greater the effectiveness."[23] Immediately I began thinking about situations that existed at the church and in our business. For the first time I understood that they were the direct result of poor leadership on my part. I needed to make some decisions I had been reluctant to make. There were some specific actions only I could take that would improve those situations. My failure to lead was holding both the church and the business back.

It was a very powerful moment for me, and it made me very passionate about wanting to improve my leadership ability. If I could raise my leadership lid, I could raise the effectiveness of both church and business. If I refused to improve my leadership ability, both organizations would suffer.

Before leaving that conference, I invested in some material I believed would help me learn how to become a better leader. I began to listen to leadership tapes, read books about leadership, and watch training videos. I made leadership development one of my goals for the new year and every year.

You may question your own leadership abilities and wonder if you could ever improve as a leader. God called you to a ministry position because He believes you have leadership potential. It is up to you to develop it.

Leadership can be learned. Poor leaders can become good leaders, and good leaders can become excellent leaders. The key to leadership development is to have a plan. There is excellent material available, but you must be willing to spend the time to study it. Your church should have money set aside in its budget for you to purchase books and other resources. If it does not, you should talk to the church about adding such money. Your growth benefits them, and they should be willing to invest in it.

As a bivocational minister you have another possible source for leadership development. Your employer may offer such programs to its employees. I took every course my previous employer offered me and found many of them to be very helpful to my pastoral ministry. Your employer may have a tuition assistance program that would pay for you to take some leadership courses at a local college. My employer's program paid for all my tuition while I earned my bachelor's degree. You, your employer, and your church all benefit from the knowledge and skills you gain from such programs.

Your leadership ability will have an impact on the success of your ministry. So will the leadership ability of those around you. This is an area of your life in which you need to continually be growing. Develop a plan by which you can grow as a leader, and map out a strategy by which you can help others around you develop as leaders also.

The Final Test of Leadership

The final test of leadership is preparing the church for your successor. We pastors must never see ourselves as irreplaceable. The time will come when our gifts and contributions will not be needed at the church we presently serve. Our churches may need different gifts than we have to achieve the next level. There will come a time when age or health concerns will lead us to retirement. God may call us into ministries different from the pastoral ministry. Regardless of the reason, a day will come when a new pastor will lead the church we now serve. For these reasons, churches should carefully plan for a smooth and successful pastoral transition.[24]

As I write this chapter, our church is going through such a transition. About a month ago I announced my resignation after serving as the pastor for 20 years. As I noted earlier, I accepted a new position with our denomination that will allow me the opportunity to work with a number of churches and be more involved in developing bivocational ministers. There is no doubt in my mind that God opened up this ministry opportunity for me and that I was the person He called to fulfill these responsibilities. However, that did not make it any easier for me to leave the church I had served and loved for so many years.

Not only did I feel called to this new ministry, but also I believed Hebron needed a pastor with different gifts than I had. The church had enjoyed numerous blessings over the years, but it needed to go to another level, and I did not feel I had the gifts necessary to lead them there. I agree with Henry and Richard Blackaby when they write, "Wise leaders also know when the time has come to exit graciously and allow a new leader to step in. Some leaders have greatly depreciated their effectiveness and diminished their contribution to their organizations by staying in positions long after their effectiveness was past."[25]

About a month before our region would make its final decision as to whom to call to this position, I informed our church deacons that it was possible I would be leaving. I wanted to ensure they heard this from me rather than from someone leaking the information that I was being considered for another position. When the decision was made, I immediately told our leadership, and the following Sunday I informed the entire church.

My message that Sunday dealt with my leaving. I explained the selection process that our region and I had gone through and my reasons for considering another position. For the next six weeks my sermons were about transition and vision. I continually tried to affirm the people and what we had accomplished over the years. I also tried to encourage them that God had even greater things in store for their future.

Prior to my leaving, the church selected a search committee to begin looking for a new pastor. The committee contacted the denominational person who would help them with this process. The committee surveyed the congregation to learn what the church wanted in their next pastor. According to the church constitution, the deacons have the responsibility for finding an interim pastor to fill the pulpit during this search process. A local minister agreed to serve as interim pastor, and the deacons filled the pulpit themselves until he could begin.

The church leaders have risen to the challenge and are providing the leadership the church needs at this time. As I write this, I have been gone from the church for almost two months, and neither the attendance nor the offerings have decreased. Never have I been more proud of the people at Hebron.

Although smaller churches may be accustomed to seeking a new pastor every year or two, they seldom change how they do it. Whether they use church boards or search committees, they follow their denomination's procedures. Yet, they often fail to ask certain key questions. When I interviewed with the pulpit committee from Hebron, I was never asked my philosophy of ministry or what I believed my spiritual gifts were. I was asked if I thought there was any hope for that little church, would we live in the parsonage, and how much money I would have to receive to serve as their pastor. Several times since, I have talked to the church about the questions they need to ask their future pastoral candidates.

Unless the pastor has been terminated from the church, he or she should spend some time helping the congregation determine what they need in their future leader. As a bivocational pastor, you can help them decide if they should stay a bivocational church or if it's time they consider calling a "fully funded" pastor. You are aware of the plans and dreams of the church, so you can make recommendations about the spiritual gifts they should seek in their next pastor that will help them achieve those dreams. Once you make these suggestions and offer advice, you must step aside and allow the church to select the person they want without any interference from you.

When I began my ministry at Hebron, I found an envelope in my desk drawer left by the interim pastor who had served the church while it sought a new pastor. Inside was a mailing list of the church members. He had written some comments (all positive) about a few of the members and indicated the ones who served in leadership positions. He included a few pictures of some church events and a brief account of the months he had spent at Hebron. This was very helpful information for me as I began my pastoral ministry, and I planned to do the same thing for my successor.

The final thing you can do for a smooth transition is to stay away from the church. The church has a new pastor, and he or she must be allowed to become the pastor. He or she needs to perform the weddings and funerals for the people of the church. Performing these activities enabled you to become the pastoral leader. The people began to trust and accept you as you ministered to them during these significant times. Allow their new pastor to gain their trust so he or she can find the same acceptance you enjoyed.

Reflections

- Who are the leaders in your church?
- On a scale of one to ten, how would you evaluate your leadership ability?
- What is your plan to improve your leadership abilities?
- What is your plan to raise the leadership abilities of those around you?
- How well do you understand the culture of the church and community in which you minister?

5 | Integrity in Your Life

The first seven verses of 1 Tim. 3 describe the qualifications for a pastor. The interesting thing about this list is that the vast majority of the qualifications have to do with the character of the person. Little is said about abilities or even spiritual gifts. The same is true in the parallel passage in Titus 1:5-9. Clearly God is very concerned about the character of those who provide leadership in the Church.

So far we have learned that the success of our ministry depends on our ability to lead our churches. We have also learned that leadership is based on our ability to influence others. Our ability to influence others is determined by whether or not they trust us. As John Maxwell points out, in order to build trust the leader must demonstrate competence, connection, and character to those he or she leads.[1] General Norman Schwarzkopf emphasizes the importance of character when he said, "Leadership is a potent combination of strategy and character. But if you must be without one, be without strategy."[2]

In a survey of 1,300 senior executives, 71 percent said that integrity was the quality most needed to succeed in business.[3] Integrity is also the key to the success of the bivocational minister. Personally, I believe it's the single most important ingredient that will determine whether the bivocational minister will enjoy a successful ministry or not. Because relationships play such an important role in the bivocational church, the pastor must have the absolute trust of the congregation if he or she is to provide leadership. If the pastor proves to not be a person of integrity, he or she will never have the trust of the congregation and will be unable to lead them.

What Is Integrity?

Integrity is living in such a way that our behavior matches our words.[4] The minister who preaches about stewardship and does not tithe to the church is not ministering with integrity. There are some pastors who claim that their ministry is their tithe to God, but I have never found biblical justification for such an attitude. No minister can expect to rob God of His tithes (Mal 3: 8) and believe he or she is serving God with integrity.

In recent years we have seen ministers disqualified from ministry because of moral failures. Publicly disgraced, they have been exposed for their lack of integrity in this area of their lives. Most of them lose the ability to lead their congregations because they have lost the confidence of their people. While some denominations provide counseling, assistance, and even restoration in some situations, few ministers who demonstrate a lack of moral integrity are ever able to serve in a ministry position again.

Charles Swindoll says, "True integrity implies you do what is right when no one is looking or when everyone is compromising."[5] Integrity is what you are in the dark when no one can see your actions. As bivocational ministers, we frequently work alone. We're usually alone when we visit members of our church. Many of us do not have assistants even in the next office when we meet someone for a counseling session. Because of our second jobs, many of these sessions are held at night. Without wisdom and integrity, we are prime candidates for moral and ethical failure. Later in this chapter I will discuss how to prevent such failure in our ministry.

Why Is Integrity So Important?

Satan knows what the impact is on a church and community

when a Christian leader fails in some area of his or her life. When some prominent television ministers failed morally several years ago, I did not want to go to my factory job. I knew the questions I would be asked. I knew the comments that would be made about hypocrisy in the Church. I also had to deal with concerns from some of our church members who had financially supported these ministries over the years. Only eternity will know the number of people who may have been turned away from God because of the lack of integrity on the part of these leaders.

Christian leaders are under tremendous temptations to compromise their values and the principles they proclaim. Satan achieves a major victory every time he can lead a minister into sin. He can destroy a minister, the minister's family, and the effective ministry of a church for years if he can just get the pastor to violate his or her integrity. We must never forget that Satan is the master deceiver (John 8:44). He will try to convince us that compromise will benefit our ministries and enable us to serve God more effectively. He will assure us that we are entitled to pleasure and personal gain because of the work we do for God.

For this reason, Christian leaders must take personal responsibility for their behavior and attitudes. We cannot conduct our lives and ministries based on what others do. Even if others appear to be compromising, we must stand firm. We cannot blame other people or circumstances for our behavior. The costs of moral failure are great, so we must be vigilant and hold fast to our integrity.

Areas of Integrity

We will now look at some specific areas of ministry and life that are especially vulnerable to compromise and failure. Integrity must be maintained in each of these areas if we want to enjoy a successful ministry.

Perhaps immorality in the area of sexual behavior has destroyed more ministers than anything else. Earlier we saw that much of the minister's work is done alone. This makes us very vulnerable to sexual misconduct.

The following scene has occurred too many times. The pastor has a counseling session with a woman who begins to share the problems in her life. Perhaps she's in a difficult marriage. Intimate details of her life are discussed. The pastor's marriage also has some rough spots. He can identify with her problems and doubts. To let her know he understands what she's going through, the pastor begins to share some of his own struggles. It doesn't take too many such counseling sessions before an emotional attachment occurs between the two of them. Suddenly they have fallen in love with each other. This may or may not lead to a sexual relationship. Even if it does not, they have still entered into an improper relationship that defrauds their marriage partners. The pastor has crossed the line and violated his integrity.

The pastor seldom intends for this to happen, of course. Although there are sexual predators in the ministry, who need to be exposed and removed, they are rare. In most cases, the pastor was simply seeking to minister to someone and inadvertently entered a situation that could destroy his or her marriage and credibility.

The wise pastor will take steps to prevent such a situation from occurring. Some of these steps are as follows:

- Never meet with a person of the opposite sex alone. If I'm meeting a woman at the church, I make sure other people will be there. Often I'll ask my wife to go to the church to practice music while I meet with the person. Because of the times in which we live, I think it would be wise for you to do the same thing when meeting with a young person of either sex. I also will not meet with a woman by myself for a meal nor ride alone in an automobile with her. Even if you are certain nothing inappropriate will happen, such guidelines eliminate even the appearance of evil (1 Thess. 5:22).

- Never share details of your marriage with someone you're counseling. If you're having marital problems, you and your spouse may need to seek help, but that help will not come from someone you're trying to help. Greater problems will come from sharing your marital difficulties with a counselee.

- Recognize when feelings for someone seem to be inappropriate. If you find yourself beginning to look for opportunities to meet someone of the opposite sex, you need to take immediate steps to end the relationship. If it's a counseling relationship, tell the person you can't provide counseling any longer, and refer him or her to another counselor.

- Understand the power of touching someone. A woman confided to her counselor that her psychiatrist would give her a hug at the end of their session. She admitted that she would then go home and fantasize about the psychiatrist.[6] While the pastor may be conveying care with a touch, the other person may misunderstand the meaning. It may be best to find other ways of expressing this care.

- Listen to your spouse. A pastor friend of mine told me of a time when his wife warned him about a woman in their church. At the end of the worship service, the pastor and his wife would greet people as they left the church. One Sunday the wife suggested he be careful around one woman. My friend laughed and accused his wife of being overly jealous and suspicious. She told him she noticed this one lady always held on to his hand a little longer than necessary, flirted with her eyes, and always took a step toward the pastor while holding his hand. The next Sunday my friend noticed this behavior on the part of this woman for the first time. Our spouses are sensitive to this sort of behavior, and we're wise to listen to their counsel.

Another area in which we need to maintain our integrity is unique to bivocational ministers. This area is our second jobs. Our employers pay us to work for them. They're not paying us to evangelize our coworkers, spend time in sermon preparation, or do telephone visitation during working hours. I have seen bivocational ministers spend more time doing ministry work than the work they were being paid to do. This is unfair to their employers, and it is a very poor witness.

I knew one bivocational pastor who had a very bad attendance record in his place of employment. His employer warned him that if his attendance did not improve, he would be placed on report. The pastor complained that the company should make allowances because his absences were related to his ministry. The employer understandably could not adjust the attendance policies for one employee. His fellow coworkers resented him wanting special favors, and many of them lost respect for him. Fortunately for all involved, the pastor soon resigned his job and became a "fully funded" pastor.

Col. 3:22-24 reminds us that as Christian workers we are working for God and not just our employers. We should give our best effort in all we do as we seek to please God. Such efforts demonstrate integrity and earn us respect from our employers and coworkers. Such respect may lead to ministry opportunities.

Integrity must also be maintained in the confidences people share with us. Few things are more disturbing to a person than to hear some personal secret shared with the pastor used as a sermon illustration. Even if we don't identify the person, that person often assumes everyone knew the pastor was talking about him or her. This is an even greater problem in the smaller churches the bivocational pastor usually serves. Everybody in the smaller church knows everyone else, their families, and many of their problems.

We need to be very careful as we address prayer concerns. Each Sunday at Hebron we read the names on our prayer list and allow people in the congregation to share prayer concerns they may have. It's one thing to ask the church to pray for someone in the hospital. It's another matter to announce that this person is undergoing treatment for prostate cancer. Such information may well have been shared with the pastor as a private matter. Disclosure could be very embarrassing to the person involved.[7] Others can pray for this individual without knowing all the details.

Holding to sound doctrine is another area where we must maintain our integrity. We live in an age of compromise, where many reject absolute truth. Some churches have compromised biblical truth to attract people. We must never be guilty of such compromise.

For many bivocational ministers the cause of this problem may be a lack of doctrinal training rather than compromise. John MacArthur is right when he writes, "Purity of doctrine is the crucial foundation upon which everything else in the Christian life rests."[8] If we want to see our church members grow spiritually, we must do everything we can to ensure we're teaching them sound doctrine.

There are many options available today to the bivocational minister who wants to develop a sound theology. Some of these options are

- Attending seminary or Bible school.
- Attending a local university.
- Taking Internet-based classes offered by a growing number of seminaries. The master's program I am taking is through a distance-learning program offered by a fully accredited seminary. I have to take only two classes on campus, and those will be taken as week-long intensives.
- Using Bible study programs developed for the computer.
- Developing a solid library of theological books written by respected scholars.

Another area where our integrity must be kept is in our honesty. Honesty and integrity go hand in hand. Jack Hayford believes that "few things are more important to the character of a leader than exhibiting absolute honesty in all communication with those whom he leads."[9]

Unfortunately, not all pastors are committed to being truthful. A pastor's wife recently wrote to a ministry complaining about her husband's habitual lying. The church had confronted him about his lies to no avail. The wife wrote, "I'm ashamed of my husband. And our children don't trust him. He preaches a powerful message, but he can't tell the truth, because he doesn't have the truth in him. . . . I am thinking of leaving him."[10] This minister had lost his integrity with his family, his church, and perhaps himself because he was not committed to being truthful.

If we want to be honest with our churches, we must also guard against plagiarism. As we prepare our sermons, we draw from many sources. We need to give credit to these sources. Sometimes a pastor will use an illustration and share it as if it happened to him or her. His credibility and integrity will come into question if someone hears another minister apply the same illustration to his or her life.

We must also guard our integrity in the area of ministry having to do with our relationships with other ministers. Bivocational ministers will seldom pastor the largest church in town. We watch other churches grow, offer exciting new programs, attract young families, and build new facilities. Our limited budgets and older facilities do not allow us to compete with these fast-growing churches. We may even lose some of our members to these other churches because of the programs they offer. This can cause a great deal of frustration to the bivocational pastor, and such frustration can lead to developing a critical spirit toward another church and its leaders.

During the early 1980s, when I began my ministry, the charismatic movement started impacting many denominational churches. Many of these churches were not open to this movement and warned their members to stay away from it. Some of those people left their churches to join other churches that were more accepting of the charismatic experience. When I met with other pastors, the conversation often included criticism of these people who left their churches and the churches that were getting these new members. The worship styles, doctrines, and leadership of these churches were also criticized. There will always be doctrinal differences between believers of different persuasions. Worship styles and music preferences will always exist between different churches. These differences do not permit us to become critical of other churches.

Jack Hayford suggests, "It just might be possible that the highest call to integrity we as leaders need to hear today is the call to love one another as we have been loved, forgiving of one another as we have been forgiven."[11] As fellow ministers serving the same God, we need to treat one another with grace and love. When God chooses to bless another church or leader, we should rejoice. When a church or leader faces difficulties, we should come alongside to pray and encourage.

The final area I will address is that of keeping commitments. Stephen Covey reminds us, "If we can't make and keep commitments to ourselves as well as to others, our commitments become meaningless. We know it, and others know it. They sense our duplicity and become guarded."[12]

When we agree to visit a church member, that person is expecting to be visited. If something happens to make visiting impossible, we need to contact that person promptly. When someone asks us to remember him or her in prayer and we agree to do so, we must follow through. More than once I've forgotten to do this, and although the person may never know, I do, and it grieves me.

I heard a story that once someone asked Albert Einstein for his telephone number, and he pulled out a piece of paper on which it was written. The person was amazed and asked Einstein if he couldn't remember his own telephone number. Einstein reportedly replied that he never tried to remember anything that he could write down and look up.

That story may or may not be true, but I've quit trying to remember everything I'm supposed to do. Write appointments down in a calendar. Purchase a daily organizer, and let it be your memory. You'll be less likely to forget important information and more likely to keep commitments you make with others.

The Integrity Process

My last two years working in the factory were spent in the quality department. One of the interesting things I learned about quality control was that quality engineers were more concerned with the process than with the final product. If the manufacturing process was right, the product would be right. Defective parts were often the result of someone not following the established process. Instead, someone took a shortcut or allowed a minor deviation in that process.

The same thing happens when a minister demonstrates a lack of integrity in his or her life. The Bible gives us the process of living a holy, righteous life that's pleasing to God. As long as we follow its teachings, we'll live our lives with integrity. The moment we deviate from those teachings, we risk losing our integrity.

A minister who becomes involved in immoral or unethical behavior did not suddenly fall into sin. At some point he or she made a choice to violate biblical teachings and his or her own conscience. The deviation may have been very minor at first, but it set him or her on a course that would eventually lead to serious problems.

We must never think we have conquered the integrity problem. 1 Cor. 10:12 warns us, "Let him who thinks he stands take heed lest he fall." The minister who believes he or she can flirt with temptation and not sin will probably have some serious integrity problems in the ministry.

The Result of a Lack of Integrity

John MacArthur states that "an essential goal for any spiritual leader is to gain the people's trust through genuine integrity. . . . But once a leader has proven to be hypocritical in any area of ministry, no matter how seemingly insignificant, he has lost everything he has labored for in ministry and sees his credibility destroyed."[13] Charles Swindoll tells us that "broken moral integrity means the spiritual leader forfeits the right to lead."[14]

How can the congregation trust a minister who lacks integrity? How can a minister the congregation does not trust lead them? Trust is such a fragile thing. It can take a lifetime to develop and only a moment to lose. Our ministries are too important to throw away for a few moments of pleasure or compromise.

When God called us into bivocational ministry, He entrusted us with the souls of those He gave us to lead. This is a wonderful privilege and responsibility, but we will stand before Him one day and give account for how we conducted ourselves and our ministries (Heb. 13:17). Let us be found faithful in our tasks and in our integrity. May we not stand before God on that day filled with shame as we remember the lack of integrity in our lives that kept us from fulfilling the ministry He gave us.

Reflections

- In what areas does Satan tempt you to violate your integrity?
- What boundaries have you established to guard your integrity when dealing with members of the opposite sex?
- How would the employer of your second job rate you as an employee?
- Are you completely honest in your dealings with others?
- How is your relationship with other pastors in your community?

Commitment

6 to Your Church

A few weeks ago, a young pastor announced to his deacons that he was resigning as the pastor of their church. Although he was only a few days away from the first anniversary of his pastorate, he felt his pastoral work was harming his seminary studies. Once again this small church will spend time searching for a new pastor rather than effectively ministering to its community. Unfortunately, this same scene occurs in small churches across the country every week.

The average tenure of senior pastors is about four years.[1] However, in the smaller churches where many bivocational pastors serve, that turnover rate among pastors is even more frequent. It's not uncommon for smaller churches to change pastors every 12 to 18 months. It is no wonder that many smaller churches find it so difficult to grow or enjoy a successful ministry.

Lyle Schaller tells us that "it is rare to find a small congregation that has experienced substantial numerical growth, *and sustained that growth,* without the benefit of a long pastorate."[2] Doran McCarty agrees: "A long tenure is necessary for success. . . . Tenure is important because it gives you the opportunity to become family . . . and gain trust as you care for their holy objects and become part of their tradition."[3] Darius Salter writes, "Pastors who are successful tend to stake their ministry on one church and one location for one lifetime. That may not be the reality of their pastoral experience, but it is their intention."[4]

Valid Reasons for Changing Churches

There are many valid reasons for changing churches. Here are a few:

- You are called to a different type of ministry.
- Your church does not share your vision for ministry.
- You have financial needs that cannot be met by your present church.
- You or your mate develops health problems.
- You learn that your spiritual gifts are a poor match for your present church.
- You serve a very unhealthy church that does not wish to change.
- You are in serious conflict with people within your church.

Please understand that none of these reasons mean you must begin looking for another place of ministry. Maybe you need to explain your vision for ministry better. Or possibly you can work out a plan to overcome your church's financial limitations. Or maybe God wants you to be the pastor who brings healing to an unhealthy church. Or perhaps you can learn how to manage conflict better. Many of these reasons can be overcome, but possibly they also indicate God does want to move you to another place of service.

The Myth of Greener Grass

The problem is that we pastors are too quick to want to move on rather than work through difficulties in our churches. We live in a world that has conditioned us to expect everything to be given to us almost immediately. I've been known to get impatient with our microwave! Because of that desire to receive everything quickly, we sometimes don't want to give God time to work in our situation. It's easier to move on to another church. We begin looking for that perfect church that will appreciate us and flourish under our leadership. We look for greener pastures while forgetting the grass is actually greener where it's watered and where someone cares enough to nurture it.

H. B. London Jr. and Neil Wiseman write, "Most desirable places were difficult until a previous pastor loved the church into greatness.

. . . This means that ministers must sink their roots where the Father providentially places them."[5] They further suggest that "many apparently unattractive and overgrown church settings are rich in opportunity beyond our wildest imagination. In many places, a bumper crop awaits the pastor who cultivates the land and plants the gospel seed."[6]

L. R. Scarbrough served as the second president of Southwestern Baptist Theological Seminary. He once challenged some spiritual leaders with similar words when he said, "If your place is not great enough to suit you, make it so. The minister who is unable to make a place great is too weak to hold a great one."[7]

I've always felt that a pastor should not begin to look for another place of ministry until he or she felt certain about leaving his or her present church. Several pulpit committees have asked if I would be willing to meet them. I usually refused because I did not feel my work at Hebron was done. If God has not called me to leave my church, why waste time looking for another one?

A few years ago, several churches looking for a pastor contacted me. During one 18-month period I received calls from an average of one church a week. A few of these churches were seeking a "fully funded" pastor, but the majority of them were bivocational. I explained to most of them that I felt no call to leave my present ministry and would not be interested in talking with them about their churches.

As churches continued to call me, I wondered if God wanted to move me to another place of service. I did agree to meet with three or four of the churches to explore that possibility. Although the interviews with these churches went well, after much prayer I felt no release to leave Hebron and asked to have my name withdrawn from consideration.

However, there were times when I wanted to leave Hebron. During times of discouragement or frustration, I would be convinced that I should seek another place of ministry. My résumé would be updated and made available. Not one church ever contacted me during those times. That only added to my discouragement and frustration until I became willing to submit myself to God's direction in this matter.

During those times when I was seeking another place of service, my ministry and the ministry of the church suffered. I felt no need to make long-range plans for the church, because I didn't plan to stay there to implement them. Sermon planning was nonexistent. Ministry was a week-to-week endeavor. The church's ministry and I were on hold, and it was a time of deadness for both of us. In contrast, when I submitted to God's will regarding my place of ministry, I committed myself to planning and preparing as if I would be my church's pastor from then on. Such commitment brings real freedom and success as God's work can once again be done.

Staying for the Long Haul

Developing a long-term commitment to our current congregations will take more than simply wanting to. It will require us to retrain ourselves to evaluate our ministries qualitatively more than quantitatively. And it will probably mean building an effective, ongoing network of support to keep us focused on our callings and to encourage us through those inevitable times of discouragement. We will need to remind ourselves that the best place is not always the biggest or even the most comfortable place. The best place is the place of God's appointment."[8]

Your definition of a successful ministry may be the determining factor as to how long you will remain at your present ministry. Bivocational ministers often serve smaller churches. If you equate success with numbers, you may not want to stay at your present ministry very long. You'll feel frustrated and perhaps even feel like a failure. You'll want to move to another church in a larger community that has a greater likelihood of growing, and your present church will once again feel the sting of pastoral rejection. Ron Klassen and John Koessler ask, "Why do so many small-town churches never seem to get beyond the survival mode? Certainly there are several factors, but the rapid turnover of pastors in these churches is one of the largest."[9]

My heart goes out to these churches. These people love the Lord and want to serve Him, but they often can't get a pastor to stay long enough to provide the leadership they need. Many of them feel abused and abandoned by the numerous pastors who have served their churches. Perhaps more than anything else, they want a pastor who will truly love them and help them in their spiritual development. When a congregation experiences that kind of love from their pastor, great things can begin to happen in that church.

One of my professors at Boyce Bible School told the story of his first Sunday as the pastor of his church. He informed the people that morning that God had called him there to love them and serve them as their pastor. He committed himself in that first sermon to do that. He remained as pastor of that church until he retired 30 years later, and the church thrived under his leadership.

You'll also have to win the battle against discouragement. Satan has few tools more effective than discouragement. Change and growth usually come slowly in the smaller church. There will be months and even years when it seems that nothing worthwhile is occurring. You may begin to doubt that God ever gave you a vision for the church.

God promised Abram and Sarai that they would have a child. Years passed with no children being born to them. They became discouraged and decided to help God's plan by having Abram father a child by his wife's maidservant. When Abram was 99 years old God appeared again to him and repeated His promise that Abram and Sarai would have a child. Although they doubted they could have children at such advanced ages, the promised son was soon born to them as God had promised (Gen. 21:2).

Their example reminds us that God's timing is not often the same as ours. God may give us a vision for our churches, but that vision may not be fulfilled for many years. Remember the saying "Mushrooms grow overnight, but oak trees take many years to grow." God wants to do great things in our churches, which can take time. If we commit to remaining in our churches longer, we'll stand a better chance of seeing this happen.

Gather people around you who can help you keep the long-term perspective that's needed. Over the years my wife has been the person who has helped me conquer discouragement. Because she knows me better than any other person, she recognizes when I am feeling discouraged about something in the church. She will begin to remind me of what God has been doing in the church. She helps me see the big picture rather than the particular object of my focus. Every pastor needs someone to provide support like this if he or she is committed to staying at a place of ministry for a long time.

What Is Needed for a Long-term Ministry?

One of the reasons pastors give for changing churches is the belief that they have taken their present church as far as they can. While this might be a valid reason, it may also be an indication that they have stopped growing as ministers. A pastor will not experience success in ministry nor enjoy a long ministry in any one church if he or she stops growing. This important subject will be discussed in greater detail in a later chapter.

A planned preaching program is also important in a long-term ministry for a number of reasons. Time management is very important to the bivocational minister, and long-term sermon planning allows more time for sermon preparation. Most of us have experienced those Saturdays when we still didn't know what to preach the following day. Planning our sermons eliminates that headache and helps us overcome the temptation to dip into our sermon barrel to resurrect an old favorite.

Planning our sermons also enables us to think about what our congregations need. If God has given you a vision to lead your church into more active evangelism, you may need to preach about evangelism and how to do it. Incidentally, our churches need these how-to sermons. If you're serving in a church that has had many pastors in a short time, your people have heard sermons about the Great Commission. They have been made to feel guilty long enough for not doing evangelism. Many of them are just waiting for someone to teach them how to do it.

Such planning also allows a pastor to bring in other resources that can be used to enhance his or her preaching. In an earlier chapter I discussed the leadership training we did at Hebron. During that time I was able to plan my sermons to coincide with that training. In addition, we added a Wednesday evening program to complement the training. Using John Maxwell's video series based on his book *The 21 Irrefutable Laws of Leadership,* we had a well-rounded program to help develop the leaders in our church. The church is still reaping the benefits of that study.

The bivocational minister must believe that God wants to do something significant in the church he or she serves. H. B. London Jr. and Neil Wiseman tell us, "Every assignment is holy ground, because Jesus gave Himself for the people who live there. Every place is important because God wants you to accomplish something supernatural there. Every situation is special because ministry is needed there. Like Queen Esther, you have come to the kingdom for a time like this."[10]

One bivocational minister began his ministry in a small church that seldom kept any pastor more than a year. Little ministry had occurred there for many years. Other pastors in the community offered him little encouragement, and the church was considered dead by many people. Even some of the members wondered if the church should close its doors. Fortunately, the new pastor believed that God would not have called him to that church if He had not planned on doing something significant in its life.

There were no great spiritual breakthroughs during the first few years, but there were little signs that God was working. Other churches occasionally contacted the pastor asking if he would be interested in serving as their pastor, but the pastor stayed where he was. After a number of years, the church began to experience revival. People were being saved. Church members became more involved in ministry. Offerings rose well above budget needs, allowing more ministry to occur.

There is tremendous excitement and anticipation in this church today.

This bivocational pastor had no special gifts or secrets formulas for success. He simply believed that God was not done with this church, and he refused to abandon it as so many others had.

Another key element to a long pastorate is a genuine love for the people you serve. Many years ago a pastor wrote in his diary, "This morning I prayed hard for my parish, my poor parish, my first and perhaps my last, since I could ask no better than to die here. My parish! The words can't even be spoken without a kind of soaring love. . . . I know that my parish is a reality; it is not a mere administrative segment, but a living cell of the everlasting Church."[11]

What a beautiful expression of love for a church! Each of us should feel this way about the church God has given us. Not only would such passion enable us to remain during difficult times, but it would also have a great impact on our people. George Barna tells us that "a key to being effective is to demonstrate love in such a way that people will realize they are significant and cared for in God's eyes."[12]

Reflections

- Do you view your present church as a permanent place of service or as a stepping-stone to a more significant ministry?
- Who are the people who help you keep a long-term perspective for your ministry?
- Does your sermon planning reflect the needs of your people and the goals and vision you have for your church?
- Do you truly love the people God has given you to serve?

7   Passion for the Ministry

Several years ago I attended a Billy Graham School of Evangelism that was held in the city where Billy Graham was conducting a crusade. During a break between sessions, I overheard a conversation between two ministers. One of them confessed that he would leave the ministry if he did not experience some type of spiritual renewal at the evangelism school. The pressures of ministry had taken their toll, and he was ready to resign. I have often wondered if God touched him during the school or if he did indeed leave the ministry.

This occurred before I began my own pastoral ministry, and I have to confess that I did not understand his feelings. I hate to admit it, but I was shocked and disappointed that someone who had been called by God into the ministry would actually think of leaving that calling because things were difficult. Believe me—after 20 years in the pastoral ministry, I'm much more compassionate toward his feelings, because I've shared them more than once.

There have been times when I felt like "Robo-Pastor." Push the button, and out comes another sermon. Pull the string, and I show up in the hospital room of a sick parishioner. Program in the dates of the church meetings this week, and I'll be there. During such times I am ministering on autopilot. There's no passion in what I do. There's no joy. Also, there's usually little success.

Fortunately, I have always been able to get over such feelings and renew my passion for ministry. During a recent sermon, I shared with our congregation again how much I enjoyed being their pastor, preparing and preaching sermons, and providing leadership and pastoral care to them. I truly love it! I wholeheartedly agree with Samuel Chadwick:

> If there is anyone in the world I pity, it is the one who has no love for his job. I would rather preach than anything else. I have never missed a chance to preach. I would rather preach than eat my dinner or have a holiday, or anything else the world can offer. I would rather pay to preach, than be paid not to preach. It has a price in agony of sweat, tears, and no calling has such joys and heartbreaks, but it is a calling an archangel might covet; and I thank God that of His grace He called me into this ministry. I wish I had been a better minister, but there is nothing in God's world or worlds I would rather be.[1]

Passion Begins with Your Call to Ministry

Do you remember when God called you into the ministry? I remember my call, and I also remember that few people understood or were excited when I told them I believed that God wanted me in the ministry. During my teen and young adult years I had strayed far from God. It was after I had just renewed my relationship with Him that I believed He had called me. I did not know what He had planned for me, but I was willing to do whatever it was.

The great minister Peter Marshall referred to God's call on a person's life as the tap on the shoulder. He wrote, "The true minister is in his pulpit not because he has chosen that profession as an easy means of livelihood, but because he could not help it, because he has obeyed an imperious summons that will not be denied."[2]

Moses was content to tend his sheep until God tapped him on the shoulder. Although he initially resisted God's call, he later distinguished himself through his passionate obedience to God's leading.

The apostle Paul was not even a Christian when God tapped him on the shoulder, but that tap led him to faith in Christ and to a magnificent ministry as a missionary, church planter, teacher, and writer. His passion for ministry is found throughout his writings and in his life:

If I preach the gospel, I have nothing to boast of, for necessity is laid upon me; yes, woe is me if I do not preach the gospel! For if I do this willingly, I have a reward; but if against my will, I have been entrusted with a stewardship. What is my reward then? That when I preach the gospel, I may present the gospel of Christ without charge, that I may not abuse my authority in the gospel *(1 Cor. 9:16-18)*.

Similar statements can be found in many of the books Paul wrote. This passion existed despite the persecution he experienced because of his ministry (2 Cor. 11:23-28). Paul knew that God had called him to the ministry, and nothing could dampen his passion for that call.

Furthermore, Paul knew he had been called to serve as a bivocational minister. While ministering in Corinth, he stayed with Aquila and Priscilla because they were also tentmakers, and the three of them worked together (Acts 18:3). In his letters to the Thessalonians, he reminded them that when he ministered to them, he met his own needs through his labor so he would not be a financial burden to them (1 Thess. 2:9; 2 Thess. 3:8).

Obstacles to Maintaining Passion for the Ministry

While passion for the ministry is essential to achieving success in it, there are many obstacles to maintaining that passion. You will encounter some of these during your ministry. Knowing what these obstacles are can help you avoid many of them. Even if you don't avoid them, it's important to recognize what is stealing your passion so that you can address the problem as quickly as possible.

A major obstacle to maintaining passion for the bivocational minister is fatigue. I remember watching *The Ed Sullivan Show* when I was growing up. One of my favorite acts was the person who would have several plates spinning on slender poles. He would start one plate spinning and then go down the line and start others. Every few seconds the first plates would start spinning more slowly, and he would have to run back to the end and get them going faster again. At the end of his performance he would have several plates spinning at the same time.

Bivocational ministry is a lot like that. We have several plates we have to keep spinning—our relationship with God; our family; our church ministry; our second job; outside interests; and ourselves. About the time we think we have all these plates spinning as we should, we notice that one of them is starting to slow down and is about to fall. We rush back to restart it and then notice others need our attention. There comes a time when we don't have the energy to keep them all going. Fatigue has set in. We wait until one plate falls off the pole before we tend to it. About the time we get it spinning again, we hear the crash of another plate as it hits the ground. Weariness replaces the passion and joy we felt when we began our ministry.

Fatigue is often a time management problem, and time management will be addressed in a later chapter. The best way to avoid fatigue is to maintain balance in each of the above-mentioned areas. I discussed the importance of maintaining balance in our lives in *The Tentmaking Pastor.*[3] I strongly encourage you to read that book and Richard Swenson's book *Margin.*[4]

There will be times when fatigue is a factor in our lives. People pick the most inopportune times to have problems that need the minister's attention. There are seasons of the year such as Christmas and Easter that demand more time from the minister. Programs such as Vacation Bible School may place extra demands on you. When fatigue may become a factor because of increased activities, it's important to respond as quickly as possible. Try to exclude some other functions. Skip a committee meeting. Schedule a guest speaker.

A few months ago, some of the singers and musicians in our church asked about the possibility of having an all-music worship service. We did this one Sunday the previous year, and it was very well received. I looked at my calendar and noticed the following month was going to be very busy. During the last week of the month I would be attending an out-of-state conference on Thursday through Saturday. Although I would be back Saturday evening, I knew I would be tired the following day. I asked our musicians if that Sunday would be acceptable for their program. They presented a very fine music program that day, and I was able to relax, enjoy the service, and not worry about having to preach after a very tiring week.

Our second jobs are often the cause of fatigue for the bivocational minister. Many of us work 40 hours a week, and some work overtime. When I began as a bivocational minister, I worked in a factory, so my hours were not very flexible. All my ministry work had to be done around my work schedule. Fatigue can quickly become a problem if we don't take care to prevent it.

The easiest way to prevent fatigue is to get plenty of rest and exercise and to eat a balanced diet. That's easier said than done. Many ministers are notorious workaholics. Who has time for exercise? Many of us consider a balanced diet as holding a sandwich in one hand and a soft drink between our legs while using our other hand to drive to our next activity. We live such a lifestyle and wonder why we feel tired so much of the time. (Incidentally, this is how I behaved for much of my ministry, and I'm working hard to improve.) We can avoid much of the fatigue that comes in our lives if we use some common sense and take better care of ourselves. Your ministry will be more successful (and probably longer) if you get the rest, exercise, and diet you need.

Another thief of ministry passion is pressure. Brooks Faulkner lists several pressure points a minister may experience:

- The pressure of preparing to speak so many times during the week
- The pressure of relationships
- The pressure to provide good content in what is said in speaking
- The pressure of counseling people who have problems bigger than we can handle
- The pressure of feelings of inadequacy

- The pressure of not having someone to talk to
- The pressure to set the pace
- The pressure to create and maintain momentum
- The pressure of being an arbitrator.[5]

Space does not allow me to address each of these, but I do want to discuss the pressure of not having someone to talk to. H. B. London Jr. and Neil Wiseman tell us, "The average pastor has few genuinely close friends. Eight out of ten pastors say they have no one to openly interact with about professional and personal concerns other than their spouse."[6]

The situation may be even worse for bivocational ministers. Due to the demands of our second jobs, it's often difficult for us to attend ministerial and denominational meetings. Many of us feel that our "fully funded" brothers do not understand bivocational ministry, so we're often reluctant to share our concerns and struggles with them. Some of us continue to feel intimidated by other ministers due to the size of our churches, our lack of a formal theological education, or our bivocational status. We're afraid of appearing stupid, so we keep our thoughts to ourselves.

Even though there are many bivocational ministers leading churches today, we're often scattered out. A bivocational friend of mine recently attended a pastor's meeting to address bivocational issues. When the bivocational ministers were asked to stand, he was the only one. As an African-American, he remembered thinking, "Now I'm a member of two minorities." It was a very uncomfortable experience for him.

Because we have few opportunities to relate with our peers, we often feel very lonely. Pressures from the demands of bivocational ministry build up inside us because we have no one to talk to who will understand. That pressure soon robs us of our passion for ministry.

We need to get proactive to overcome this problem. Start by overcoming your sense of being a second-class minister because you're bivocational. Choose some ministers in your area you feel you can trust, and begin to share your concerns and struggles with them. They'll probably be more understanding than you thought.

Contact your denominational office to find other bivocational ministers in your area. Set up a meeting with them. Perhaps your denominational office could help you have such a meeting. This may become a regular meeting where you can encourage and support one another.

Check the Internet for some bivocational resources. One of my favorite sites is one maintained by Philip Yang that provides a forum for bivocational ministers to ask questions and share ideas with one another. You can be a part of this group by sending an E-mail to <bivopastor@aol.com> and asking to be included in the discussion group.

Do not allow loneliness to steal your passion. Search out people with whom you can share. Make friends with other people both in ministry and outside ministry. Find people who can support you and who need your support in return. You will enjoy a much more successful ministry if you do.

A lack of results can also rob you of your passion for ministry. It's not easy to work hard, sacrifice, and follow the vision you believe God has given you for the church and then see few results for your efforts. You begin to question your call to the ministry. You wonder if you should consider another church that might provide better results. You lie awake nights wondering what you're doing wrong.

There are many reasons you may see few results in your ministry that have nothing to do with you:

- Your church has seen rapid pastoral turnover for a number of years.
- Your church has been plateaued for many years, and it will take time for it to build momentum for significant growth to occur.
- Your church is composed of members who oppose change.
- Your church is in an area of little or no growth in population.
- Your church is affiliated with a denomination that's not well known or accepted in the community.
- Your church is not healthy.

- Your church has a bad reputation in the community.
- Your church needs a pastor with different spiritual gifts than you possess.

One or a combination of these problems can limit the effectiveness of your ministry. The good news is that all of these problems can be resolved. The bad news is that it's going to take time.

Pastors always dream of the perfect church. We pray to be led to a church where the members are inviting new people to attend church with them every week, the sanctuary is full of people taking notes of every sermon we preach, and the front of the sanctuary is packed with lost people responding to the invitation to receive Jesus Christ as Lord. We yearn for a church where the weekly offerings always exceed the budget needs, more people volunteer to teach than we have classes, and where every business meeting runs smoothly and effectively.

Such a church only exists in our dreams. We're called to minister to real churches made up of real people. Because we're imperfect people, our churches are also imperfect. Unfortunately, some churches have serious problems, and these problems must be resolved before these churches can have an effective ministry to others. While you may not be responsible for these problems, God may have called you to a church because you're the person He wants to use to promote healing in it. This is why it's so important to discover what God's vision is for a church.

Perhaps our lack of results is due to our trying to fulfill our vision of what we want to accomplish rather than God's vision. Pastors attend conferences and return to their churches excited about what they've learned. The conference leaders share how their programs have led to significant growth in their churches, and we're convinced that we need to introduce the same programs to our churches. We promote these programs, invest time and resources in them—and watch as they do nothing for our churches.

Several years ago our church decided to bring a youth minister on staff. The community surrounding our church was filled with young people, but none of them attended church. We determined that we needed to start a youth ministry in an effort to reach these young people and their families. Money was included in our budget for programming and to pay the salary of someone who would lead our youth program.

Other churches in the area were amazed that a church our size would have two paid staff people. Our average Sunday morning attendance was approximately 50 people. I explained to all who asked that one of the advantages of having bivocational ministers is that money for additional staff is more readily available. We called our first youth minister and launched that ministry with great anticipation.

During the next few years we had a succession of youth ministers. Some were excellent leaders who worked very hard to build a youth program. Despite their best efforts, we never achieved a youth program that effectively reached out to the young people in our community. The youth ministers, our church, and I were consistently frustrated by our lack of success. Our last youth minister stayed with us for two years trying to build a solid program but was unable to do so. When he resigned, the church decided to drop the idea of a youth ministry.

At the time we blamed many factors for our lack of success. Looking back on it now, I believe we were attempting to do something that was not part of God's vision for our church. Perhaps we were ahead of God's timing, and one day He will lead Hebron to begin a youth ministry. If that happens, the church will find that their efforts will produce much more effective results.

Restoring Your Passion for Ministry

Fatigue, the pressures of ministry, and a seeming lack of results can all rob you of the passion you once felt for ministry. They can even lead to burnout and cause you to leave the ministry. The good news is that you can overcome these difficulties—if you choose to do so. Andrew Blackwood wrote, "In pastoral work the most serious obstacles lie within a man's soul."[7] How we choose to respond to the problems we encounter in ministry will determine whether or not we minister with passion.

As bivocational ministers, we must do two things to maintain our passion for ministry. First, it is essential that we reconnect with God's original call on our lives. We will know our share of problems and disappointments in ministry. Our critic's voices will wound our spirits. In time, the difficulties of ministry can make us forget that God has called us to ministry. We must peel back the onionlike layers of problems until we rediscover God's calling.

It's also important to remember that God called us to bivocational ministry. We should not allow ourselves to become envious of ministers who lead larger congregations or appear to have more successful ministries. Bivocational ministry is not inferior to "fully funded" ministry. God calls some to serve as bivocational ministers and others to serve as "fully funded" ministers. In 2 Tim. 1:9, Paul reminded young Timothy that "[God] has saved us and called us with a holy calling, not according to our works, but *according to His own purpose and grace* which was given to us in Christ Jesus before time began" (emphasis added). Perhaps one day God will change your calling and lead you to a "fully funded" ministry position. Or he may allow you to serve as a bivocational minister throughout your entire ministry. Rejoice in God's call on your life no matter what it may be, and you'll find it easier to maintain passion for your work.

Second, we need to maintain our passion for Jesus Christ. As ministers we spend so much time studying about Christ and teaching others about Him that we run the risk of neglecting our own relationship with Him. Ministers need to heed the warning the apostle John gave the church at Ephesus. Good works and sound theology are important but not enough (Rev. 2:1-7). We must not neglect our personal relationship with the Lord.

While attending Bible school, I realized I was learning much about God and how to do ministry, but my relationship with Him was suffering. All my reading was either for preparing sermons or for school assignments. My prayer life was weak as well. I found that other students were experiencing the same problem.

I wish I could say that I never experienced that problem after graduating from school, but I still find that my personal devotional life suffers from time to time. I have looked back at my prayer time and found that my prayers that week were all pastoral, not devotional. I may have prayed for individuals and needs that had been shared with me, but I did not spend much time in worship and giving thanks. When my devotional life is weak, I spend little time reading for personal growth. Over the years I have found that my passion for ministry is directly proportionate to my passion for Christ. Thus it is important to my personal growth and my ministry success that I maintain a healthy devotional life.

We spend time doing those things we believe to be important. A devotional life does not usually just happen by accident. We need to make it a priority and set aside time for it.

I try to begin each day by reading two small devotional booklets. Our church provides the devotional book *Our Daily Bread* to our members, and I find it to be a helpful part of my devotional time. I also read a similar booklet published by Promise Keepers titled *Men of Integrity*. For the second year in a row, I'm reading through the Bible in a year with *The Daily Walk Bible*. I conclude my devotions with prayer.

This past year I rediscovered the importance of having a Sabbath. I was preaching a series of sermons through the Ten Commandments and became convicted as I prepared my sermon about honoring the Sabbath. Scripture does not say, "Remember the Sabbath day, to keep it holy unless you are a minister." I became very aware that I never took a Sabbath day to rest and reconnect with God. Sundays were busy at church, and I spent Monday through Saturday mornings at our family business. The afternoons were times for study, visitation, and sermon preparation.

That week I decided I would begin to take a Sabbath day on Mondays. During my sermon the following Sunday, I shared my struggle with our congregation and told them of my decision. I encouraged our church not to call me on Mondays unless it was an emergency. I asked the same thing from my office administrator at our business. Both have honored my request.

I did not want Mondays to be a day off where I played golf, fished, or worked around the house. I wanted this to be a true day of rest and re-connection with God. In good weather I sit on our back deck and read while enjoying the beauty of God's creation. I spend time praying and writing. Occasionally I'll take a nap. One Monday I decided to visit a friend in a neighboring community who was instrumental in my salva-tion and my early growth as a Christian. We had not seen each other for a couple of years. I called his church office, and we met for a leisurely three-hour lunch in which we laughed about our early days of working together in a factory and talked about how God was blessing our church-es. I left that lunch refreshed and my passion for ministry renewed.

When I worked in the factory, I could not take a day off as I do to-day. Every bivocational minister works different schedules and has dif-ferent job requirements, but I encourage you to find some time in your schedule for a Sabbath. You not only need the rest but also the time to reconnect with God and refuel your passion for Christ.

You may have found other ways to maintain a close, personal re-lationship with God. The best methods are those you have found to be meaningful to you, so don't think you should copy mine. Just be sure that your busy schedule as a bivocational minister does not rob you of a vibrant, passionate relationship with Him.

Reflections

- What do you remember most about the time you first felt God's call on your life?
- How do you prevent fatigue from taking away your passion for ministry?
- What are the greatest pressures in your life or ministry? How are you responding to them?
- What are you doing to maintain a passionate relationship with God?

8 Faith in God

The apostle Paul challenged the Christians in Galatia about abandoning the grace of God and replacing it with a theology of works. He asked, "Are you so foolish? Having begun in the Spirit, are you now being made perfect by the flesh?" (Gal. 3:3). A similar question could be asked of many bivocational ministers. Having begun our ministries with the belief that God called us to minister, do we now try to fulfill that call through our own power and might? Unfortunately, too often we do.

Bivocational ministry is tough enough. It's even more difficult when we try to do it on our own strength. Although a strong, gifted leader may be able to lead a church for a time through his or her own efforts, it will be a much more difficult task and will produce fewer results than if he or she depended upon God. H. B. London Jr. and Neil Wiseman are correct when they write, "In pastoral routines, it is easy to forget that ministry at its core has a supernatural linkage with the resources of God. Although most pastors can preach, counsel, visit, comfort, raise funds, and lead without divine enablement, everyone does it better with God's help."[1]

We must constantly depend upon God for success in our ministries, but there are two times it is especially important to maintain our faith in Him. One is during times when everything seems to work against us, and the other is when we are enjoying success.

During Difficult Times

We all have times when we wonder if our work and effort is worth it. After spending hours preparing a sermon, it's hard not to be disappointed when many of our members choose to be elsewhere that Sunday. We can become frustrated when we see our church membership remaining the same year after year despite our best efforts to grow the church. Other churches are growing. They're starting exciting new ministries that are impacting their communities. We wonder, "Why is my church unable to have a dynamic youth group or a great-sounding choir?"

John Maxwell talks about a leadership law he calls the "Law of the Big Mo."[2] He describes how difficult it is to stop a train that's rolling down the tracks, and yet that same train can't even start with a one-inch block in front of its wheels. For many of us bivocational ministers, our churches have stood still for so long that it seems as if we'll never get them moving. We're caught in a vicious circle: People don't want to attend our churches until we have the programs they're seeking, and we can't begin programs without the new people who want them.

I remember a visit I made several years ago to a family who had not attended church for many years. They had a problem with their old church and had dropped out. With four sons, they admitted they needed to return to church. I encouraged them to visit Hebron. They asked about our youth program. I responded we did not have a youth program but that with their sons attending our church, we would start one. They said they would not attend a church that did not have an established youth program. I left that visit frustrated, wondering how we could have a youth program if we couldn't get youth to attend our church first.

Many bivocational ministers lead older, established churches that may have plateaued many years go. Some may be close to shutting their doors. As ministers, we don't want that to happen. We believe that God still has a purpose for our churches, and we're willing to work hard to help them grow. Amazingly, we may run into a brick wall with our congregations. They resist the programs we believe will help their churches grow. There's little interest in reaching out to the unchurched surrounding communities. Our members may be more interested in preserving their past than in looking to the future.

I recently spoke with a bivocational minister who had been at his church for eight months and was already considering looking for another pastorate. His church did not want to do anything to grow or reach new people. Although he loved his congregation and believed that God had called him to that place of service, his frustration with their apparent lack of interest in growth was causing him to look elsewhere.

I counseled him that he should not give up so quickly. Eight months of ministry is not a long time in a church. He had not yet earned the right to lead these people in new programs. They still needed to learn to trust him and be certain of his love and commitment toward them. If he truly believed that God had led him to this church, he needed to trust Him for the results. Rick Warren tells us, "Don't worry about the growth of your church. Focus on fulfilling the purposes of your church. . . . God will grow his church to the size he wants it, at the rate that's best for your situation."[3]

This is why we must take the long-term approach to our ministries. Seldom will we see the results we would like to see as fast as we would like to see them. A church in a difficult situation did not get in that position overnight, and it's unlikely to climb out quickly. Certainly God has a plan for your church, but it may take time to accomplish. We must remember that God is in charge of our churches. We must obey and trust Him for the results. As Leith Anderson reminds us, "We participate in God's sovereign processes and results, but we do not determine them."[4] Remember the words of the apostle Paul: "Let us not grow weary while doing good, for in due season we shall reap if we do not lose heart" (Gal. 6:9).

To me, the key words in that verse are "if we do not lose heart." More than once I have been tempted to lose heart. I have had times when I so wanted to move to another church that I would have taken anything just to get away from where I was serving. There have been other times when I was tempted to leave the ministry completely. Thank God I never did either one, or I would have missed out on the many blessings that later happened when God touched our church and my life.

George Barna studied several churches that went from decline to growth. He writes this about their pastors:

> Turnaround pastors were unusually devoted to seek an intimate relationship with God on a regular basis. It appears that the severity of the circumstances of the church pushed these leaders into a deeper state of submission and dependence upon Him than is found in most church settings.
>
> A realistic assessment of most of these churches, of course, would have led to the conclusion that there was no hope of breathing life back into the limp body. With that in mind, these leaders invariably recognized that the only true plan was to rely fully on Him for strength, wisdom, grace, guidance, and power.[5]

Maintaining your faith in God is the only way to deal with the many difficulties that occur in ministry.

> Above all and everything else, the pastor needs always to remember that he is not alone in his work. If God called him, God's Spirit will be with him and help him. Lay it all before the Lord; tell him about it; seek his face and divine wisdom. He has answers we never thought of and ways of solution we never dreamed of. Pray and pray and pray. God will answer and answer. Always the pastor's greatest resource is God.[6]

During Good Times

Maintaining our faith in God may be even more difficult when things are going well in our churches. During these times there is great temptation to credit some new program we have started in our church. If the church begins to grow numerically, we may claim it is due to an evangelistic or outreach program we implemented. If the offerings increase, we may think it is due to a stewardship emphasis we introduced in our church. We can also be tempted to think our success is because of our great preaching or leadership skills.

I recently attended a two-day conference for the company my family owns. The subject was how to structure a company to be more profitable. The conference leader was well known and respected in the industry. He had turned an average company into one of the nation's leading companies in its field and won a national award for his efforts. A few years later, he sold his company for several million dollars and became a consultant and conference speaker.

Many of the ideas he presented were good, sensible ideas. I returned home planning to implement some of them. He seemed to be a decent human being, but he had an air of arrogance I found hard to get past. He talked of his hard work, his drive, and his impatience for anyone who got in his way. He enjoyed telling us about the rewards of his success—a new Mercedes, $300 shoes, a yacht, and several vacation homes. Not once did he ever acknowledge any role God had in his life.

As I returned home from that conference, I thought about some pastors I had met, both "fully funded" and bivocational, who were like that man. They talked about the great things they had done in the ministry. They described how they pushed their agendas through their church boards and committees. They enjoyed telling others about their perks. Seldom did they acknowledge the blessing of God on their ministries or even the hard work of their church members.

A sure sign that pride has taken root in leaders' lives is that they lose compassion for those they are leading. When leaders become calloused to the hardships of their people, their pride has desensitized them. When leaders impose financial cutbacks and hardships upon their people, yet they continue to shower lucrative benefits upon themselves, they forfeit their prerogative to lead. Leaders who become preoccupied with their own personal accomplishments, and are oblivious to the needs of others, are not worthy of the call to lead. Pastors who are unmoved when a church member is hurting, or who are ambivalent when one of their flock falls by the wayside, are abusing the privilege of spiritual leadership.[7]

Reflecting further, I thought about how easy it is for me to be just like this. I enjoy attending pastors' meetings when good things have been happening at *my* church. (Isn't it funny that it's *my* church when things are going well and *our* church when things are in a slump?) I love to talk of our successes at Hebron, and I believe it is good to do that. The church needs affirmation that it is doing well, and other churches can be helped by hearing that God is at work in our churches. The danger is in the temptation to take credit for the good things that are happening.

Has there ever been a pastor who has not been tempted to take the glory that belongs to God alone? We must remember that God will not share His glory with anyone else. We can introduce new programs into our churches, visit people seven nights a week, and prepare the greatest sermons that have ever been preached, but God chooses what He will and will not bless. Without His blessings on our ministries, we are doomed to failure.

I believe that if we attempt to take the glory that rightfully belongs to the Lord, He will remove His blessing from our ministries. It's almost as if He says to us, *All right—you want to take the credit for how things are going in the church; I'll remove My hand and presence from the church, and we'll see how well things go solely through your efforts.* Do any of us really want that to happen? I certainly don't, because I know how things would go, and I don't want to put the church through that.

Charles Stanley tells us,

> It is only when we identify the object of our faith that we truly know the foundation for our success. If you put your faith in yourself and your abilities, intellect, and dreams, then your foundation is only as strong as you are. And no matter how strong you may be, you are neither omnipotent nor omniscient. If you put

your faith in God, then your foundation is as strong as He is, which is all-powerful and all-knowing.[8]

How do we make sure God receives the glory He is due? While I enjoy the compliments and positive comments I receive from the church when things are going well, I try to make sure I give those to God. Not only will I remind people that God is the One who is blessing our work, but also in my prayer time I will offer up to God those positive comments as properly belonging to Him. This is not false piety but an honest acknowledgment that God alone deserves our worship and praise. We need to remind ourselves of the words of Jer. 45:5—"Do you seek great things for yourself? Do not seek them." If we seek great things for God and His kingdom, we will enjoy much greater success as bivocational ministers.

Encouragement for the Bivocational Minister

You may or may not have the education you wish you had. Your church may be a small, struggling church in the foothills, a poor urban church, or a new church plant trying to get started. You may be serving a church that once had a great ministry, but those days went away long ago as the church declined. At times it may seem to be an impossible task to juggle the needs of the church, the demands of your second job, and the family and personal needs you have. Remember this: your faith in God allows you to draw upon His limitless resources. Hudson Taylor once wrote, "All God's giants have been weak men, who did great things for God because they reckoned on His being with them."[9]

I encourage you to meditate on that statement, especially if you're feeling overwhelmed with life and ministry. Maintaining confidence in God's call on and provision for your life and ministry can enable you to enjoy a successful ministry. Let me close this chapter with a word from John Frye.

Pastor, on the brink of or neck-deep in your ministry, do you live in the confidence that God knows you, calls you by name and is with you? Do you find strength in the truth that he knows *the deep you* with whom you are perhaps out of touch or of whom you are unaware? Do you depend on and find courage in the truth that Jesus is also called "Immanuel"? God is with you! One of the primary promises giving life and courage to the pastoral task is this promise of divine presence. "I am with you always, to the very end of the age" (Matt. 28:20).[10]

Reflections

- What have you found to be the most discouraging aspect of your ministry?
- Have there been times you were tempted to "lose heart" in the ministry? What sustained you during those times?
- Have you had times when you took the glory belonging to God for a success in the church? How did God convict you of that, and how did you return His glory to Him?
- Who or what is the object of your faith?
- Reread Hudson Taylor's comment. How do his words make you feel?

9   Growth of the Minister

By now you should understand that I view a long-term ministry to be essential to the success of a bivocational minister. Years of faithful service allow a level of trust to develop between the minister and the church. This trust enables the church to take risks it would not otherwise take. It can start new ministries that can more effectively reach the community. A high level of trust between the congregation and the pastor creates an attitude within the church that God is doing something significant.

Unfortunately, that same trust can also cause the church and pastor to become satisfied with the victories they have enjoyed. Everyone settles down into a comfortable routine. That routine can quickly become a rut, and a rut is best defined as a grave with the ends knocked out. There is not much life around a grave. There is also not much life in such churches.

Bivocational pastors can quickly settle into such a routine. Our church members understand that we spend a certain number of hours at our second jobs. As long as we preach reasonably decent sermons and provide a measure of pastoral care to our church members, most of them will be satisfied. Unfortunately, some of us in bivocational ministry will be satisfied as well. We shouldn't be. Franklin Segler reminds us that "mediocrity is one of the worst sins of the pastorate. If the church is ever to mature in Christ, it must have the example and challenge of mature leadership."[1]

Being bivocational does not license us to provide second-rate leadership. God does not have one standard for a "fully funded" pastor and a lower standard for the bivocational minister. He expects every person called into ministry to fully use the gifts He has given to provide excellent ministry to the church.

If we want to enjoy a successful ministry, we must be committed to regular growth. As usual, John Maxwell is right on target when he writes, "As you prepare to take the success journey, there is an essential activity that only you can perform for yourself. . . . That activity is preparing and pursuing a personal growth plan."[2]

Almost every profession requires their members to be involved in continuing education. The reason is simple—change.

The average life span for a person living in North America today is longer than it was 30 years ago because of new information and improved medical technology. But what would happen if a doctor graduated from medical school in 1970 and never read a journal, took additional classes, or pursued continuing education opportunities? His patients would be treated with 30-year-old medicines and procedures. Those patients would not enjoy the benefits of all that has been learned in the past 30 years.

Change also occurs in the church. Two decades ago, door-to-door visitation was an effective means for a church to connect with its community. Many people today view such uninvited visitations as intrusions into their busy lives. A number of years ago the Sunday evening service was primarily evangelistic. Most churches that still have a Sunday evening service today use it for training their faithful church members. Volumes are being written about the changes taking place in church worship and music.

Perhaps the greatest challenge facing the church today is understanding how unchurched people think and feel about the church and Christianity. I gave my life to Christ as a young man in my mid-20s. But

I regularly attended church as a child and during my teens. I knew the language of the church, and although I had not personally applied them to my life, I believed the truths of the Bible. When my pastor and Christian friends talked to me of my need to accept Jesus Christ as Lord and Savior, I understood what they were saying, and I knew they were right.

Many secular people today were not raised in the Church. They do not speak the Church's language, nor do they trust its teachings. They do not believe the Church is relevant to their problems. Even worse, many believe there are many ways to God besides Jesus Christ and that a person should be allowed to pursue God in his or her own way.

Because of all the changes taking place in the Church and society, ministry is becoming more challenging and only growing ministers will be successful in the future. Steve Bierly, a small-church pastor, warns us, "If you are not trying to grow as a pastor, you won't be able to retain even the level of competence you have now."[3] John Maxwell notes, "Change is inevitable. . . . Growth is optional."[4] However, it is not optional for those who want to enjoy a successful ministry.

The remainder of this chapter will examine four specific areas where most pastors need continual growth. Please note that these areas are all practical skills pastors use every week, not spiritual disciplines such as prayer, study, meditation, and worship. Spiritual growth has been addressed in another chapter, and although it is absolutely essential for a successful ministry, God also expects us to use the gifts and skills He has given us. These are our tools for ministry, and tools must be sharpened and maintained to be effective. Every bivocational minister can become more successful when he or she grows in these areas.

Relational Skills

John Maxwell tells an amusing story from his first pastorate. He quickly learned that one of the laymen in his church was its real leader. Anything this layman presented to the church was immediately approved. Maxwell developed a relationship with this person and would suggest to him things that needed to be done. At the next church meeting the gentleman would present the idea, and it would be approved. Maxwell enjoyed a successful ministry in that small rural church because he developed relationships with the members and worked through those relationships.[5]

Most bivocational churches are relationship oriented.[6] Failing to build relationships with the members, especially the lay leaders, will often result in a short, disappointing pastorate. However, taking the time to build those relationships can lead to a very effective ministry.

How do we build these relationships? For some ministers, the first step is to come out from behind their desks and spend time with their people. "Leaders must live where their people live, feel their emotions, and intuitively sense their thoughts."[7]

As bivocational ministers we may have an edge in this area over "fully funded" ministers due to our second jobs. We live and work in the same world as our members. We have firsthand knowledge of the anxiety people experience when the contract is up between the factory and unions. We understand how the family is impacted when slow sales mean small commission checks. We know how draining it is to work eight hours a day alongside a coworker who ridicules our Christian beliefs and frequently blasphemes the name of the God we love so much.

Although we may better understand the world where our members live, the challenge for bivocational ministers is to relate individually to our members. With all the demands on our lives, where do we find the time to visit our members so we can better understand their personal issues? The answer is that we will not find the time—we must make it.

The second step in relationship building is to listen to the members of your congregation. Dale Carnegie said, "You can make more friends in two weeks by becoming a good listener than you can in two years trying to get other people interested in you."[8]

People appreciate someone who will listen to them. We live in an impersonal world where much of our communication is with answering machines, fax machines, and E-mail. These may make us more productive and effective, but they don't help us relate to one another. When we're afraid, hurting, confused, or frustrated, we want to talk to a real person with emotions and feelings like ours. We want someone to actually listen to our concerns.

A few years ago a newspaper story told of an individual who started a new business. For a fee, he would listen to people on the telephone for 30 minutes. He provided no advice; he just listened. He advertised his services in a few newspapers, and his telephone soon started ringing. People were willing to pay a fee just to have someone listen to them.

Listening to our church members can be one of the most helpful ministries we provide. Our challenge is to be active listeners. We need not only to listen to the words they use but also to try to understand the emotions behind the words. We need to read body language, ask questions, and clarify anything that might be misunderstood.

Being honest and transparent with our church members also helps build relationships. Our people experience joy and pain, courage and fear, hope and disappointment in their lives. They enjoy wonderful victories and experience disappointing defeats. They struggle with temptations, doubts, and questions about their faith. We in the ministry need to let them know we experience the same things in our own lives.

Ministers are not immune from temptation. Like the members of our churches, we are human beings who need God's forgiveness. We must not be afraid to admit this to our church members. Certainly, we must be discreet and avoid the sensational, but our honesty about our own humanness will strengthen our relationships with our members.

Ministers also sometimes struggle with questions about their faith. A bivocational friend of mine was conducting evangelistic revivals and was active in his church when a close relative passed away. Rather than supporting my friend and his family in their time of loss, his fellow church members criticized them for lacking faith. My friend and his wife were devastated by their attitudes and left the church for many months. Their faith in God was nearly shattered. Eventually they returned to a different church, and today he is the bivocational pastor of an active and growing congregation. His openness about his trial of faith enables him to relate to others going through similar crises.

Leadership in a bivocational church is directly related to building relationships with the members of the church. Growing in relational skills leads to a more successful ministry.

Leadership Skills

If it is true that everything rises and falls on leadership,[9] then growing in this skill is essential to a successful ministry. Since leadership is discussed in another chapter, here we will only examine growth in leadership.

The question is often asked, "Are leaders born or made?" The correct answer is both. Certainly, some people are born with more natural leadership attributes, just as some people are born with greater musical abilities.

Even the most musically challenged person (such as me) can improve his or her musical skills with practice, while a few with great musical gifts can play beautiful music while in grade school. However, even the most gifted musicians know they must continue to grow and practice if they want to keep improving. Great cellist Pablo Cassals was heard practicing when he was well over 80 years old. Someone asked him why he continued to practice at his age, and he answered, "I think I'm noticing some improvement."[10]

Each of us in bivocational ministry should desire to see continual improvement in our leadership skills. We need to expose ourselves to sound leadership training. John Maxwell's material on leadership development has had a powerful impact on my life and ministry. He has helped me identify strengths and weaknesses in my leadership skills, and as a result, I believe I am growing as a leader.

We should also associate with others who have excellent gifts in leadership. As we observe their lives, we learn how they respond to the challenges and opportunities they encounter. We can seek their counsel about matters we're facing in our own lives. This type of mentoring from leaders we respect will help us grow in our own leadership abilities.

Communication Skills

When we think of growing as communicators, we must discuss both our public and private communications. Our public communications involve our preaching and teaching responsibilities. Private communications include witnessing, counseling, meeting with small groups such as committees and church boards, and mentoring. Successful ministry demands continual growth in both areas.

Nothing the bivocational minister can do has the potential to impact a church more than his or her pulpit ministry. John A. Broadus wrote in 1870, "The record of Christian history has been that the strength of the church is directly related to the strength of the pulpit. When the message from the pulpit has been uncertain and faltering, the church has been weak; when the pulpit has given a positive, declarative message, the church has been strong. The need for effective preaching has never been greater."[11] John MacArthur agreed with Broadus when he wrote, "No man's pastoral ministry will be successful in God's sight who does not give preaching its proper place."[12]

The apostle Paul asked, "If the trumpet makes an uncertain sound, who will prepare himself for battle?" (1 Cor. 14:8). Pulpit ministry enables the pastor to sound a clear message to his or her congregation. In preaching the pastor can cast vision, teach doctrine, and challenge, inspire, and encourage the church. The results can be a more unified church with a clear purpose. Both are essential to a successful ministry.

Developing our preaching ministry requires a great deal of discipline for the bivocational minister. Prayer, planning, study, and preparation are key elements to a top-quality preaching ministry. Each of these requires time, and time is the aspect of our ministry we all battle. Thus, we must see the importance of our preaching and make it a priority.

For those who have not had the opportunity for formal training in sermon preparation and delivery, I would strongly recommend investing in some good books on the subject. Two books that have helped me are *On the Preparation and Delivery of Sermons,* a classic written by John A. Broadus, and *Rediscovering Expository Preaching,* written by John MacArthur and faculty members of The Master's Seminary.

These books will lead you step by step in developing your sermons. They describe the different types of sermons, how to select sermon text, how to effectively use illustrations, and the best ways to deliver your message to the congregation. Using the information you will learn in these books will make anyone a better preacher.

Graduates of seminary and Bible schools need to take a periodic assessment of their preaching skills to make sure they are not developing bad habits. We can do this by reading good books or articles on preaching and by listening to excellent communicators such as Charles Swindoll and John Maxwell.

Some ministers do a good job of preparing sermons, but their problem is delivering those messages to the congregation. Poor grammar and distracting mannerisms in the pulpit can take away from an otherwise excellent sermon. Usually we aren't aware we have problems in these areas. It may be helpful to record some sermons and listen to them. Ask others to critique your grammar and delivery. Don't become defensive if they point to some areas in which you can improve. Appreciate their input, because it can help you become a better communicator.

A few months after beginning my ministry at Hebron, a church member approached me. She assured me that she did not want to insult me, but she was concerned that my poor grammar would be a hindrance to ministry. While people at Hebron probably would not be bothered by it, other places of ministry might have different expectations. I sincerely appreciated her constructive criticism.

Shortly after that meeting I enrolled at Boyce Bible School (now Boyce College). Two semesters of English grammar were required for graduation. This class was taught by one of the best teachers I've ever had, and knowing my deficiencies in this area, I worked hard to improve. While no one will ever mistake me for an English major, I now preach with much more confidence.

I had an opportunity to use my newly learned grammar skills the following year. I was invited to deliver the baccalaureate message to my daughter's high school graduating class. Several thousand people were in attendance, including many of my former high school teachers. Without improving in this area, I could have embarrassed my daughter, our church, and myself. Instead, it was a wonderful experience I will never forget.

You may serve a church of 25 people who couldn't care less about the grammar you use, but that does not mean God may not have other plans for your future ministry. Don't allow poor language skills to limit your ministry or distract from your message. If you have problems in this area, take a class at a nearby college or find someone to tutor you.

Annoying mannerisms in the pulpit can also distract your listeners. Examples include speaking in a monotone, never looking at the audience, and inserting "uhs" (or the more spiritual "Praise the Lord") as transitions from one thought to another. These are often the result of being poorly prepared or nervous, and the speaker is usually not aware of such distractions.

Again, it is helpful to ask someone to point out such problem areas. For instance, my wife tells me she can tell if I get nervous while preaching, because I start rubbing my mustache. Now that I am aware of it, I try to be very sensitive of any movement toward my mustache.

Experience will help most people overcome nervousness in the pulpit. Taking a public speaking course at a local college can also be a big help. Whatever you do to eliminate these distractions will help your pulpit ministry be more effective.

Our interpersonal communication is not only with individuals but also with boards and committees. Counseling, visitation, witnessing, mentoring, and the meetings we have with various groups within the church are all included. Although our public communications will primarily be verbal, our interpersonal communications can be verbal or nonverbal. Facial expressions, gestures, and voice inflection can communicate as well as the words we use.[13]

Although public communication involves preaching and teaching larger groups of people, there may or may not be opportunities for discussion in such settings. In contrast, personal communication usually will involve discussion between the participants. Thus, the skills needed to be effective in our private, interpersonal communications are different than those needed in our public ministry. Such skills as listening, giving and receiving feedback, nonverbal communication, persuasion, assertiveness, and conflict management are some that will lead to more effective interpersonal communication.

"I know you believe that you understand what you think I said, but I am not sure you realize that what you heard is not what I meant." This is a humorous illustration of interpersonal communication at its worst. Poor communication can lead to confusion, indecisiveness, and bad decisions. As pastors, our leadership depends on our ability to properly communicate with others in the church. We can't effectively counsel, minister, or lead others if we can't properly communicate our thoughts to them. With this in mind, I have adopted two simple rules:

- The message received is the message sent.
- I am 100 percent responsible for the message received by the other party.

These rules place the responsibility for effective interpersonal communication on my shoulders. If someone misunderstands something I have said, it's my fault, not theirs. Because successful ministry depends on the ability to communicate effectively, the minister must take responsibility for doing this.

Growth in this area can occur in a number of ways. Bookstores and libraries usually have many books on interpersonal communication. Courses can be taken at a community college, but don't confuse public speaking courses with ones dealing with interpersonal communication. Also, a study of how men communicate differently from women would be helpful to many ministers.

Conflict Resolution Skills

A humorous story tells of a man who had been marooned on an island for several years. One day a man on a passing ship saw his signal fire and sent a boat to investigate. The landing party found a man standing near three buildings. When asked about the buildings, the man answered, "That building is my house, and the second building is the church I attend." "What's the third building?" he was asked. "Oh, that's the church I used to attend."

While this story may make us smile, conflict in the church is not funny. Churches split, pastors are terminated, and the work of Jesus Christ suffers when conflict is not managed properly. The pastor who enjoys a successful ministry will be one who continues to grow in the area of conflict management and resolution.

Some churches are more conflict prone than others. Keith Huttenlocker suggests six characteristics of churches that may be more prone to conflict:

1. *High exchange.* People in these churches spend a great amount of time together. These are often smaller churches located in small communities. Many of the people in these churches may be related. These are often the churches with bivocational pastors.

2. *High expectations.* Some churches have very high expectations, especially for those in leadership. Occasionally these expectations are beyond the ability of the leadership to meet. If the expectations are known, the pastor may be able to negotiate and adjust unrealistic expectations. Unfortunately, these expectations may be unspoken. People assume the pastor knows what they expect, and conflict develops when those expectations are not met.

3. *High involvement.* Conservative and smaller churches expect their members to be involved in the life and work of the church. Involved people expect to have input into the decisions of the church. They have invested their lives, their money, and in some cases their personhood into the church. Such people are simply trying to protect their investment. Sometimes these people become very possessive of "their church," and conflict results.

4. *Low trust.* Many things can lead to low trust in a church: short-term pastorates, failing to keep confidences, lack of integrity in word or action, poor attitudes. In such churches almost every proposal will be questioned. Conflict is unavoidable.

5. *Low understanding.* Some people lack good communication skills and don't understand common courtesy. Their lack of tact creates pain for others that often leads to conflict.

6. *Low respect.* This primarily refers to a lack of respect for leadership. Many today do not accept biblically based authority. In such churches the pastor is often viewed as a hired hand. A pastor asked a parishioner why she did not go to the trustees with her complaint of a burned-out lightbulb in the ladies' restroom. She responded, "That's what we pay *you* for." The pastor soon resigned.[14]

When conflict does occur, there are three basic ways we can respond. We can try to avoid it, we can try to manage it, or we can try to resolve it.

Avoiding conflict allows the problems to remain unchanged, and unhealthy patterns are permitted to continue.[15] Refusing to deal appropriately with conflict often leads to even more serious conflicts in the future.[16]

Conflict management understands that not every conflict will be resolved. We manage conflict when differing parties find ways to relate to one another despite their differences.

Conflict resolution should be our goal. Resolving conflict will lead to a healthier church and ultimately a more successful ministry. Unfortunately, resolving conflict can be difficult and sometimes messy. Many bivocational ministers have received little training in conflict resolution. For some of us, the only conflict resolution skills we have learned have been in our second jobs. Our only model may be hearing the boss resolving conflict by saying, "This is the way we are going to do it. If you don't like it, feel free to look for another job." Trying this method in our church will usually result in our looking for another church! There are better methods of resolving conflict in our churches.

Perhaps the most important thing to remember is that conflict in the church is not new. In Acts 15 we read of a council that met to determine if Gentile converts had to be circumcised and follow other Jewish customs. There was "much dispute" in this council regarding these issues (v. 7). Later in the same chapter we read of a serious disagreement between Paul and Barnabas regarding the role John Mark would have in their ministry. "The contention became so sharp that they parted from one another" (v. 39). Paul also had a conflict with Peter for refusing to eat with Gentiles when Jews were present. Paul accused Peter, Barnabas, and other Jews of hypocrisy because of their treatment of the Gentiles (Gal. 2:11-18).

The church consists of imperfect people who have been redeemed by Jesus Christ. They are in various stages of spiritual maturity and have different ideas about the best ways to achieve the goals and dreams of the church. As a result, there will always be the potential for conflict in the church. Charles Cosgrove and Dennis Hatfield suggest that "the best way to manage conflict is to treat it as something normal and bring it out in the open where it can be handled fairly and constructively."[17]

Conflict is not only normal but sometimes also helpful to the church. While I still do not enjoy conflict, I have learned that sometimes it can bring benefits. Keith Huttenlocker lists four such benefits. He writes that conflict can

1. Break up stagnant and unproductive ways of thinking and doing things.

2. Open up channels of communication between individuals.

3. Broaden the base of input and support.

4. Generate new approaches to challenge and opportunity.[18]

It is also essential that we understand that others are hurting as much as we are during conflict.[19] Perhaps a few people enjoy conflict and division, but most people feel a measure of pain. Emotions such as anger, guilt, anxiety, and frustration may be present. People may fear that they're in danger of losing something important to them. It's very important that we treat with respect those with whom we are in conflict.

Having said that, in order to resolve a conflict there will have to be a confrontation. "Confrontation is unavoidable in conflict and resolution. What may be avoided are the adverse results of unkind or unwise confrontation. Conflict does not divide us; our failure to respect one another in conflict is what divides us."[20] Jim Van Yperen adds, "The goal of confrontation is always gentle restoration, always for health, never for harm."[21]

Confrontation should open doors of communication between all the involved parties. Remember that communication includes both speaking and listening. It is important that each side truly listens to the concerns of the other. Sometimes conflicts end when misunderstandings are cleared up.

It is also essential that the discussions focus on the issues and not on personalities. Everyone loses when church conflicts result in personal attacks. Such attacks resolve nothing and do great harm to the Body of Christ. We must concentrate on finding solutions for the problems that created the conflict.

Several years ago I read that we should never waste a good crisis. The same could be said of conflict. If we're going to go through a conflict, we should seek to learn from it. As ministers we often seek to fix the problems quickly and move on. Sometimes this is a mistake. Certainly we want to resolve the conflict, but we should also seek to learn from it. Such an approach allows us and the church to grow and mature. From my observations, I see that some churches experience one conflict after another because they never take the time to really resolve a conflict. They quickly apply a Band-Aid to it, pronounce themselves healed, and move on. Soon another problem knocks the Band-Aid off, and then they have two conflicts. Leas writes, "Encouraging the others to join with you in dealing with the conflict and encouraging the other to stay with you in the process is perhaps the single most important conflict management skill one can use."[22]

To grow in our conflict management and resolution skills, we must understand our conflict style. Several years ago I took a test that revealed my primary and secondary methods of dealing with conflict. My primary style was a 1/9, which meant I was more interested in protecting relationships than achieving goals. That did not surprise me. What did surprise me was that my secondary style was a 9/1. This meant I could become somewhat ruthless in getting my way if my primary style did not seem to work.

This was made strikingly clear to me in an activity I participated in after the test. All test-takers were divided into groups of three for a role-playing exercise. One person acted as an observer while the other two tried to resolve a conflict. After the exercise, each person was critiqued. My partner stated that everything went well in our attempt to resolve our conflict until I suddenly did a complete turnaround in my attitude. She admitted to feeling some fear even though we were just role-playing. Our observer confirmed everything my partner said.

I was shocked by their comments, but I could not dispute them. I needed to learn better methods of resolving conflict so I would not come across as threatening or intimidating to anyone. In the test I took, a 5/5 would be considered ideal. This would indicate an equal interest in protecting relationships and achieving goals. Since that class, achieving a 5/5 in conflict situations has been my goal. Had I not learned my conflict styles, I might still handle conflict in unhealthful ways.

In this chapter we've discussed four areas of growth. You've probably thought of additional areas in which you need to grow. At this point it may seem overwhelming. As a bivocational minister, how will you ever find the time to grow in so many different areas? It becomes less overwhelming when you realize this is a lifelong process. Just as success is a journey, so is personal growth.

John Maxwell gives ministers who wish to grow 10 principles to follow:

1. Choose a life of growth.
2. Start growing today.
3. Be teachable.
4. Focus on self-development, not self-fulfillment.
5. Never stay satisfied with current accomplishments.
6. Be a continual learner.
7. Concentrate on a few major themes.
8. Develop a plan for growth.
9. Pay the price.
10. Find a way to apply what you learn.[23]

As we close this important chapter, let me highlight the second statement in Maxwell's list: Start growing today. Don't put it off. Determine an area or two in which you need to develop, and find resources that will help you grow in those areas. If you're not sure what those areas may be, pray about it. Ask your spouse, church board, close friends, or denominational leaders for their input. You and your ministry will enjoy much greater success as you commit yourself to a life of growth.

Reflections

- What changes do you see your church needing to make in the next year? Five years?
- How will you lead those changes?
- How would you describe your personal relationship with your church's lay leaders? What can you do to make those relationships even better?
- What improvements can you make in the way you communicate to others?

- What is your conflict management and resolution style?
- What two areas of your life and ministry do you need to grow and develop further?
- What is your plan for continual growth?

10 Equipping the Laity

"The modern church stands in dire need of a true theology of the laity."[1] These words were first penned in 1960, but they remain true to this day. Many churches, large and small, do not have a correct theology of the laity. Too often, pastors are wearing themselves out trying to do the ministry of the church while laypeople sit in the pews scoring their pastors' efforts. Such ministry is not only seldom successful but also unbiblical.

Eph. 4:11-12 reads, "He Himself gave some to be apostles, some prophets, some evangelists, and some pastors and teachers, for the equipping of the saints for the work of ministry, for the edifying of the body of Christ." The King James Version of the Bible inserts a comma after the word saints in this passage. Such punctuation indicates the ministers in verse 11 have a threefold task:

- "The equipping of the saints"
- "The work of ministry"
- "The edifying of the body of Christ"

Nearly all commentators now agree that the comma after the word "saints" should be eliminated.[2] John MacArthur explains why:

> The study and teaching of God's Word takes time. The evangelist or pastor-teacher therefore cannot fulfill his God-given responsibility if he is encumbered with the planning and adminis-

tration of a multitude of programs—no matter how worthy and helpful they are. . . .

. . . No matter how gifted, talented, and dedicated a pastor may be, the work to be done when he is called to minister will always vastly exceed his time and abilities. His purpose in God's plan is not to try to meet all those needs himself but to equip the people given to his care to meet those needs.[3]

The greatest challenge facing many pastors today is getting more of their members involved in ministry. According to Rick Warren, "Fifty percent of all church members have no interest in serving in any ministry."[4] He goes on to write, "Your church will never be any stronger than its core of lay ministers who carry out the various ministries of the church. Every church needs an intentional, well-planned system for uncovering, mobilizing, and supporting the giftedness of its members."[5]

Some bivocational ministers do enjoy an advantage in the area of lay involvement. Because the pastor has a second job, the church members understand he or she cannot always be available. These understanding lay leaders assume responsibility for visiting those in hospitals, nursing homes, and homes. There were times when the deacons in our church would visit someone in the hospital before I even knew the person was admitted. Such laypeople are a wonderful blessing to the pastor and a valuable asset to the church.

Other bivocational pastors are not so fortunate. They are still expected to do all the ministry in the church. No one is willing to minister to the sick and hurting. No one takes responsibility to contact visitors and invite them back. These are seen as pastoral responsibilities, and they expect the pastor to do them. Why would such people have such a limited and unbiblical view of ministry? Sometimes it's the fault of the pastors.

Some bivocational pastors struggle with delegating ministry to laypeople. Most of us entered ministry to serve others. We want to be involved in the lives of our members. Not only do some of our members expect us to visit them every time they are sick or hurting, but that's our expectation as well, and we work very hard to meet it.

The Example of Moses

Moses is a good example of the leader who does not delegate ministry to others. In Exod. 18:13 we read, "And so it was, on the next day, that Moses sat to judge the people; and the people stood before Moses from morning until evening." Moses was trying to do everything for the Israelites. His father-in-law, Jethro, immediately sensed that this was not good for Moses or the people. He said in verse 18, "Both you and these people who are with you will surely wear yourselves out. For this thing is too much for you; you are not able to perform it by yourself."

Jethro recommended that Moses should train others to help him. "And you shall teach them the statutes and the laws, and show them the way in which they must walk and the work they must do (v. 20). Moses followed that advice, and in verse 26 we read, "So they judged the people at all times; the hard cases they brought to Moses, but they judged every small case themselves."

Everyone benefited from this arrangement. Moses no longer had the burden of meeting all the needs of the Israelites. The people could have their concerns addressed quickly. A number of Israelites received additional training and had the opportunity to use their gifts and abilities to serve the people.

Each of us should follow Moses' example. As pastors we find that there are some things we must do, but there are other ministry areas we need to delegate. Are there people in your church with gifts of healing and mercy? Allow them to call upon some of the people in the hospital. Do you have people with speaking gifts? Why not allow them to preach occasionally?

The deacons in our church recently voted to conduct two lay Sundays a year during which they would be responsible for every aspect of the worship service, including the sermon. They also decided not to schedule these when I would be away on vacation. They reasoned

- It would give me a little break from having to prepare sermons for those weeks.

- I would be able to critique their sermons and delivery, which would help them become better communicators.
- Laypersons in the church would get experience that could be helpful if the pastor left, became sick, or was unable to minister for a period.
- The laypersons would be able to supply other churches in the surrounding area if there was a need.
- The experience may help someone recognize a personal call of God to the pastoral ministry.

Why We Don't Delegate Ministry to Others

One reason we're reluctant to delegate is that it's simply easier and quicker to do it ourselves. We often believe we don't have the time to train our laypeople to do ministry.

Although Moses recognized the wisdom of Jethro's advice, he may have wondered how he would find the time in his already hectic life to train others to judge the people. Obviously, he looked long-range and understood that the extra time he spent training others would be beneficial to him and the nation of Israel in the future. We need to take that same long-term perspective.

Whether or not we have read *The Tyranny of the Urgent,* many of us in bivocational ministry live it. Urgent things, many of them good and positive, often so fill our lives that we can't do what's necessary to provide more long-lasting benefits. Robert Raines expresses the problem well:

> The clergyman's abiding frustration is that in doing the many things that are useful, he may be prevented from doing the one thing needful. It is being suggested here that the one thing needful in the role of the clergyman for our time is that he prepare his people for their ministry in the church and in the world. The chief task of the clergyman is to equip his people for their ministry. All his work is to this end. The functions of preacher, prophet, pastor, priest, evangelist, counselor, and administrator find their proper

places in the equipping ministry. The purpose of this ministry is that the people shall be trained and outfitted for their work in the church and in the world.[6]

Church Growth Requires Delegation

If we want to grow our churches, we must learn to delegate ministry to other people. Bob Russell correctly points out that "you grow the church, not by adding people to the bottom of the pyramid and forcing the top guy to minister to more people, but by adding more circles of ministry inside the encompassing circle of the church."[7] Refusing to do this will result in the church peaking out at 150-200 members because those are all the people the pastor can care for.[8]

The bivocational pastor will not be able to care for that many people. Time constraints may reduce that number to 50-100 people for the average bivocational pastor. Since it is unlikely that the typical bivocational church will have the resources to add additional staff, it is imperative that laypeople be equipped to do ministry if the church is serious about growth.

How Do We Equip Laypeople?

So far we have seen that equipping the laity for the work of ministry is the biblical role of the pastor and that such equipping is vital to the church's spiritual and numerical growth. The obvious question is "How do we do this?"

The first step is to help the laypeople understand how important it is for them to be involved in ministry. Many Christians continue to believe that the pastor is hired to do the ministry of the church. We need to teach them that scripturally it is our responsibility to teach them how to do ministry. We also need to understand that changing that attitude may take some time.

You will probably find the 80/20 rule in effect in your church. About 20 percent of your congregation will understand the need for their involvement in ministry and will commit themselves to the training they need. Others in the church may also understand the need, but their levels of commitment will vary. Twenty percent of a congregation of 50 people will give you ten people who want to grow and be involved in ministry. Identifying these people is cause to celebrate! Now it's time to pour your life into them.

I must sound a word of caution here. This can get tricky. Church members sometimes become concerned if the pastor seems to spend more time with some of the members than he or she does with others. Those who feel they are being slighted are usually the ones who complain. Rumors begin to circulate in the church that the pastor has his or her "favorites" and that the needs of the other church members are being ignored. To avoid such criticism, most pastors try to spend an equal amount of time with all the church members.

This is a mistake for the bivocational pastor who desires to train church members to do ministry. Such an equipping pastor will need to spend about 80 percent of his or her time with the 20 percent who want to be trained. That only leaves 20 percent of his or her time for the remaining 80 percent of the congregation. This will probably generate criticism, but such criticism may be the price the pastor must pay to be successful at equipping the saints for ministry.

Jesus is an excellent example of a leader who pours himself or herself into a small group of followers to better develop their potential. We know there were many who followed Jesus. In Luke 10:1 we read that Jesus sent 70 disciples out to minister in various places. Out of all His followers He selected 12 to receive the most instruction. From that 12 He selected an inner core of three—Peter, James, and John—to be with Him at special moments. They went with Jesus on the Mount of Transfiguration while the others were left behind (Matt. 17). When Jesus entered the Garden of Gethsemane to pray before His arrest, He left the other disciples behind and took the same three into the garden (Mark 14:32-33).

Every church member is important and deserves attention and ministry, but we must invest more of ourselves into those who want to be trained for ministry. These are the people who will help the church grow.

Some Christians want to be involved in ministry but believe ministry is limited to a few special people. They can't believe that God could use them to minister. Our second step in equipping church members is to help them understand that God wants to use all His children in ministering to others. We must help them see themselves in ministry.

Viktor Frankl tells us, "If you treat people to a vision of themselves, if you apparently overrate them, you make them become what they are capable of becoming. You know, if we take people as they are, we make them worse. If we take them as they should be, we help them become what they can be."[9]

We have to find ways to help people understand that we believe in them even before they have proven themselves. That is the only way we will encourage them to reach their God-given potential. One way to do this actually leads to the third step in this process. We need to teach what the Bible says about spiritual gifts.

I remember the smiles of some in our congregation when I first taught that every Christian has at least one spiritual gift (1 Cor. 12) and that their gifts were given to them by God to be used in ministry. A few people told me later that they doubted they had even one spiritual gift.

Recently I took the teaching of spiritual gifts one step further. Using some material from John Maxwell, I taught on each spiritual gift on Sunday mornings. The Sunday morning following that series, each person was given a spiritual gifts survey and a response sheet. When it was time for me to preach, I announced I had good news and bad news. The good news was that I was not preaching that morning. The bad news was that they were free to leave when they finished the questionnaire!

Please understand—I did not unexpectedly spring this questionnaire on the congregation. At the start of each sermon in this series I reminded them we would be taking the survey. Scheduling it on Sunday morning was my way to emphasize its importance. Following that Sunday I met with those who took the survey to let them know which spiritual gifts the survey indicated they had.

I am convinced that a church's ministry success will be in direct proportion to how many of its members use the spiritual gifts God has given them. However, we cannot expect our people to use their gifts if they have not identified them and been placed in positions where those gifts can be used.

Some of us in ministry are guilty of complaining about the lack of commitment of our church members. Sometimes the problem is not a lack of commitment on their part—rather, it's a lack of instruction on our part. If I stand in the pulpit and complain about the church's lack of growth and its lack of lay involvement in ministry but do nothing to help the people identify and exercise their spiritual gifts, I am at fault. I am also at fault if I don't try to match the ministry needs of the church with those who have the gifts to best meet those needs.

Some churches have a nominating committee to fill the various positions in the church. Often some people will be asked to take a position in an area in which they're not gifted. Such people are almost doomed to failure. Despite their best efforts, their ministry in that area will not be as successful as it could have been if they had served in a ministry for which they were gifted. These are the church members most likely to burn out and to decline the nominating committee's future requests for service. Matching the gifts of the church members to the proper ministries can easily solve such problems.

John Maxwell reminds us that "anyone who continually has to work in areas of personal weakness instead of personal strengths will not stay motivated. If individuals have been grinding away at tasks assigned in their weak areas and you reassign them to work in areas of strength, you'll see a dramatic increase in natural motivation."[10]

What does the bivocational pastor do if the church is not interested in learning about or using the spiritual gifts of its members for ministry? Read some strong words from Charles Swindoll:

If you happen to be in a church that, in spite of your efforts to delegate the workload, is not sustaining itself with the gifts within it, then may I be so bold as to suggest that you deliberately teach on spiritual gifts. Willingly delegate the workload. If you find the board and flock unwilling to share the responsibilities of ministry, perhaps you should consider moving on to a ministry that allows such gifts to function. I'm of the opinion, though it may sound like heresy, that some smaller churches constantly struggling to exist ought to be shut down—or merged so that they might survive, thrive, and get a quality job done. One exhausted man's struggle to keep everything afloat is not a church,—it is a tragic story in unbiblical futility.[11]

These powerful words will disturb some people, but I wholeheartedly agree. Some bivocational ministers have spent years trying to lead a church that doesn't want to be led and trying to grow a church that doesn't want to grow. Whipping a dead horse won't make it go any faster. It's much better to get off that dead horse and find one that wants to run. If we find we're in a dead church that's not interested in life, we need to move on to one that's eager for someone to lead them.

Once we help our people identify their spiritual gifts, we need to help them grow in the areas of their giftedness. God gives each Christian at least one spiritual gift, but it's the responsibility of the individual to develop and improve that gift. The time we ministers invest in helping our members develop their gifts will have a great impact on our churches.

Please read these encouraging words slowly: "If many people in your organization improve themselves even slightly, the quality of your whole organization increases. If a few people improve themselves a lot, the potential for growth and success increases due to the increased leadership of these people. And if both kinds of growth occur as the result of your enlarging, hang on, because your organization is about to take off!"[12]

Isn't that what we want in our churches? Most people in bivocational ministry want to see their churches take off. We hunger to see people brought to a personal relationship with Jesus Christ. We want to see broken lives and broken families restored by the healing touch of God on their lives. We pray that those who have been beaten down by life will find renewed hope from a fresh touch of God. While we do see the occasional victory, we don't see them often enough.

Hopefully, by now you know that the key to seeing more such victories is to have more of your people involved in ministry. We've looked at some of the steps we can take to better equip our members for ministry. But there's still a problem. Each of these steps requires time from us that we may not feel we have to spend. We cannot stop doing ministry while we train others to do ministry. People in hospitals and nursing homes will need to be visited. Families and individuals having problems will need counsel. Church visitors need a follow-up visit. The administration needs of the church cannot be ignored. Where will we find the time to do the ministry that must be done now and train others so they can do ministry in the future?

Never Do Ministry Alone

In his church leadership conferences John Maxwell admonishes pastors never to do ministry alone. If you're making a hospital visit, take someone with the gifts of mercy or faith with you. Let him or her watch you minister and pray for the patient. This person already possesses the gifts necessary to do such ministry; he or she just needs the experience. Take someone with the gifts of evangelism or hospitality with you when you follow up with someone who visited your church. There will be times when it's not appropriate to take someone else with you, but whenever possible do ministry with other people. This allows you to meet existing ministry needs and mentor others who will later be able to do such ministry themselves.

When Billy Graham announced he would hold a crusade in a nearby city, I invited one of our church members with strong leadership gifts to attend the public announcement of the crusade with me. I wanted our church to be involved in this crusade, and I planned to ask him to lead this effort. I wanted him to catch the excitement of the crusade for himself.

Too often we pastors attend such events by ourselves and wonder why our people are not as excited about the event as we are. We need to allow them to experience these events for themselves, feel the passion of the speakers and organizers, and catch a personal vision of the difference such events could make in the life of the church.

We also need to provide resources to those who want to further develop their gifts and ministries. Such resources may consist of videos, books, or short studies we can lead. Most ministers receive advertisements in the mail about many resources that may be appropriate. Denominational offices may have excellent resources available at little or no cost to the church. This can be a great help to a smaller church that may not have much money available for such resources.

The next step in this process is to release the people for ministry. Just as Jesus sent His disciples out to do ministry, we must free our people for ministry. This involves at least two things.

Some of our people want to minister, but we keep them busy doing committee work or tasks outside their area of giftedness. Bivocational ministers should know better than anyone that our people have a limited amount of time they can spend doing church work. If someone has a strong gift of evangelism, I don't want that person serving on the pastor relations committee, the church decorating committee, and mowing the church yard each week. I want that person free to minister in the area of his or her gift. Each of these other activities may be important, but not for this person. His or her greatest contribution to the church and the kingdom of God will be in sharing his or her faith with those who do not yet have a personal relationship with God.

The other thing we can do is to bless new ministries our people may feel led to start. I have told our church members that if they believe God wants them to use their gifts in ministries our church is not currently doing, then let me know. I will bless them and provide whatever resources and help I can. This could be the start of an exciting new ministry for our church, and I want our people to feel free to explore those possibilities.

The final step is to celebrate the ministries of our people. Rick Warren writes, "You bring out the best in people by giving them a *challenge*, giving them *control*, and giving them the *credit*."[13]

Everyone enjoys recognition for a task well done. Such recognition costs very little and yet can be a tremendous encouragement. Some simple methods of recognition include

- Positive statements from the pulpit
- Mention of activities in the church newsletter or bulletin
- Thank-you cards personally written and signed by the pastor
- Telephone calls
- Invitation to a meal with the pastor
- Appreciation dinner for all those involved in ministry

Such recognition lets the people know they are important to the church and its ministry. This is a great motivator and is vital for the ongoing success and growth of the church.

Reflections

- How many members of your church are involved in ministry?
- How much ministry are you willing to delegate to other people?
- What plans do you have for equipping your people for ministry?
- How many of your people are working in the areas of spiritual giftedness? Are changes needed? How will those changes be made?
- How will you recognize church members who are involved in ministry?

11   Management of Time

At every bivocational conference I lead, the attendees are given index cards and asked to write down their biggest challenges as bivocational ministers. Without exception, every card returned to me includes the problem of time. They want to know how to find the time to lead the church, work their second jobs, spend time with their families, and have some time for themselves. These ministers understand that their effectiveness as leaders depends upon their ability to manage their time.

Henry and Richard Blackaby confirm this:

> The most inefficient and unproductive leaders have as much time as history-making leaders. Each is constrained by the need for sleep, food, exercise, and family concerns. Everyone encounters financial issues, unforeseen circumstances, and daily pressures. The difference is that wise leaders refuse to allow life's demands to control their schedule or their priorities. Unwise leaders succumb to extraneous pressures and enticements surrounding them and never accomplish all God intends for them. Great leaders don't allow their busy lives or their vast responsibilities to overwhelm them. Rather, they become the masters of their schedules through determined and conscientious effort.[1]

Herb Miller clarifies this a little more for us. He writes, "Time management is rarely a church leader's major challenge. *Priority management is the real issue!* . . . Ministry effectiveness requires sound 'priority hierarchy' judgment: Which tasks should come first at a given moment—ahead of all the others?"[2]

Setting Priorities

How do we establish priorities for all the tasks we need to do? We answer that with another question: What are our goals? Once we understand what we want to achieve, we can then determine what activities will help us achieve those goals. These activities are given higher priority over others.

John Maxwell encourages us to separate activities into four priority categories.

1. *High Importance/High Urgency:* We need to tackle these projects first.
2. *High Importance/Low Urgency:* We need to set deadlines for completion and get these projects worked into our daily routine.
3. *Low Importance/High Urgency:* We need to find quick, efficient ways to get this work done with little personal involvement. These activities should be delegated to other capable people.
4. *Low Importance/Low Urgency:* This is busy work that often takes too much of our time. Maxwell suggests stacking this work up and doing it in half-hour segments each week, letting somebody else do it, or simply not doing it at all.[3]

The key to doing this successfully is that you must be the person who decides which category each activity goes in. When other people approach you with their pet projects, they always see those projects as top priority. Although it may be a top priority for them, it may not be for you. You must determine that for yourself.

A bivocational friend of mine scheduled a vacation for his family. Airplane tickets were purchased and hotel reservations confirmed. Two weeks before the vacation, he realized the church had rescheduled its Vacation Bible School for the same week. He called the VBS director and explained the situation. Although Vacation Bible School is an important event in many small churches, his personal involvement was minimal. It was not urgent that he be there, so he and his family enjoyed their vacation.

A few years later, this same pastor and his wife left for a week's vacation. Upon arriving at their destination, they received a telephone call telling them his mother had been taken to the hospital for tests. It would be at least two days before the results would be known. A few hours later, the church board chairman called to inform the pastor that a church member had passed away. The family had made arrangements with another minister to do the funeral service, but the chairman knew the pastor would want to call the family. Before calling them, my friend and his wife decided to return home. They felt a sense of high importance and high urgency to return and be closer to his mother and to minister to the other family. Their vacation could be taken another time.

Other people were involved in the process, but the pastor determined the priority each activity was given. In the first situation, the need for him to attend a program in which he was minimally involved was secondary to the need to take his family on vacation. However, in the second circumstance, vacation, although he was already at his destination, was less important than being with his mother and the other family.

Very rarely will the priorities we assign to activities be permanent. Priorities often change and must be constantly evaluated.[4] A good example of this is preparing for a meeting that is three weeks away. You may spend some time gathering information for this meeting, but it probably won't be a high priority. However, as that meeting date approaches, it will increase in importance. A day or two before the meeting, it may consume a great deal of your time as you finalize your preparation for it.

Another example of changing priorities for bivocational ministers occurs when our second job requires us to attend a training program away from our homes. Generally speaking, we would usually place our families and our ministries before our second jobs. However, if that employer requires us to attend a two-day training event in another state, we will leave our families and our church work behind and concentrate on the training. We do this because one of our goals is to work to better support our families and to continue to serve our churches. Attending this training event becomes a high priority for these two days.

Managing Yourself

Ted Engstrom tells us that "managing our time really means managing ourselves. We have to budget our time just as carefully as we have to budget our money."[5]

Our use of time is really a stewardship issue. Each of us has 24 hours in a day. We can use those hours wisely or unwisely, and those are the only two options we have. We cannot save any of those hours and carry them over to the next day. At the end of the day they are gone forever. This is why the person who wants to be a good steward of the time God has given will schedule each day to its maximum effectiveness.

Hyrum W. Smith is cofounder of Franklin Quest, which sells the Franklin day planner. Multitudes of people use this planner to guide their schedules. Smith encourages us to "view a daily plan as your ticket to success."[6]

I have found a daily planner to be essential to managing my life. I can immediately check for available dates, track contacts, schedule events, and schedule activities I need to complete for future events.

While writing this section, I received a telephone call from an individual in a church who needed some information. After we discussed the situation, he told me he would relay this information to the church and would call me to come and discuss it in more detail later. This phone call was recorded in my planner as soon as I hung up the telephone. The caller's name, date, and nature of the call were all recorded. I do not have to depend on my memory or worry about losing a piece of paper with notes about this conversation.

There are a number of daily planners available today. Some are rather expensive, while others are less costly. You can also choose between paper planners and electronic ones. The cost of the electronic planners has dropped significantly, making them much more affordable. Although many time management experts teach that we should use only one calendar for our planning, I prefer using both a paper system and a Palm Pilot.

I find that my paper planner allows me to quickly record information and record notes. Daily tasks can be recorded, quickly reviewed, and checked off when completed. This system also allows me to easily scan both monthly and daily calendars and immediately know what's coming up and keep meeting information, telephone records, and active projects in one notebook. I can also record information in this planner much more quickly than I can in my electronic planner.

However, it's not always convenient to carry my planner to every event. The Palm Pilot fits into my jacket or pants pocket and gives me quick access to my calendar. It also enables me to print out a monthly calendar on the computer for my wife. This makes it easier for her to keep up with my schedule. Changes can easily be made, and an updated calendar can be printed. I also prefer the address feature on this device, because more information can be recorded about the people I need to contact than I could record in my paper planner.

Some might not want to take the time to record information in both systems, but I find the redundancy to be more of an asset than a problem. It doesn't take more than a few minutes a day to ensure the information is recorded in both. I have not only the benefits already described but also a backup in case I lose either one.

Managing ourselves also includes being gatekeepers of our schedules. Jeff Woods is correct when he writes, "Whether we realize it or not, we do have control over our own agendas. Others may make demands upon us as leaders, but we choose which demands to act upon."[7]

Bivocational ministers must learn how to say no to people. When we complain that our schedules are too full, we forget that we agreed for all these items to be on our schedules. We are the ones who failed to build some breathing room into our calendars.

I recently violated my own advice about saying no to people. As a result, my calendar for one month showed only two days I did not have something scheduled. That month I spent more time in hotel rooms than I did in my own home. As a result, I was exhausted and not very effective by the end of the month. I am again being much more careful about what I schedule and agree to do.

Unfortunately, there are ministers who seldom take a day off. They certainly would never think of taking a vacation. They spend little time with their families. Even if they do schedule an activity with their families, a telephone call from a church member can ruin it.

Unexpected emergencies do occur that require the minister's presence, and most ministers will respond appropriately to those situations. However, not every emergency claim is a true emergency. I like the sign I've seen on people's desks: "A lack of planning on your part does not constitute an emergency on my part."

Before our calendars become filled with activities, we need to reserve days for relaxing, reading, and spending time with the family. When true emergencies occur, we can respond to them. Otherwise, we can spend those days recharging ourselves physically, mentally, and spiritually.

As much as possible, I schedule my day off to coincide with my wife's day off from her job. We spend that day together doing things we want to do. We normally get away from the house to be free from the telephone, fax, and computer so we can truly enjoy the day together. These days are recorded in my planner weeks in advance. If someone wants to schedule a meeting or an activity on that day, I can honestly tell them I already have a commitment.

"Leaders understand that their daily schedule primarily reveals two things: those things they have chosen to do and those things they have chosen not to do. Every decision to do one thing is at the same time a choice not to do a dozen other things."[8]

When we determine our goals and the steps required to achieve them, we can then determine what activities will go on our schedule. We should choose to do those things that will help us reach our goals and exclude other activities that may not. Doing this will help us be wise stewards of our time.

Sharpen the Axe

Eugene Griessman tells the following story:

The first day the young lumberman cut down ten trees. His axe was keen, and he was strong and fresh. The second day, he worked just as hard. In fact, he felt that he worked even harder than the first day. But only eight trees fell.

Tomorrow, he would get an earlier start. So he retired early and the next morning worked as hard as he could but managed to cut down only seven trees.

The following day, he was down to five trees. The fifth day, he managed to chop down only three trees and was exhausted by nightfall. Early the next morning, he was chopping furiously when an old man passed by and asked, "Why don't you stop and sharpen your axe?"

"I can't. I'm too busy chopping down trees," he replied.[9]

Most bivocational ministers I know work hard. We start early and work late. We try to squeeze as much into each day as possible. The mistake some of us make is that we don't take time to sharpen our axes. We don't renew our spirits, our minds, or our bodies. Eventually, we will find that we're running on empty. Too many ministers have their ministries cut short because they kept chopping trees with a dull axe.

Sharpening the axe means we take time to regularly do some type of aerobic exercise that helps strengthen the heart and improves our endurance. While most people agree on the importance of exercise, few actually do it, because they don't feel they have the time. However, those involved in a regular exercise routine report that they have greater energy, are more alert, and actually accomplish more.

Sharpening the axe requires us to take time to read and think. It's important that we not confine our reading to ministry-related themes. As bivocational ministers, we may have an advantage here because most of us have to read in the area of our second careers. We often need to attend training classes related to those careers. These help stretch us and give us greater ability to think creatively about issues or challenges we encounter in ministry.

Sharpening the axe certainly includes taking the time to pray, meditate on scripture, and listen to God. It's ironic that ministers can become so busy that they have no time for these things, but I've seen it happen in my own life more than once. Other ministers have admitted having the same problem. Our ministries will be much more successful when we allow God's grace and presence to flow through us to those we serve.

It takes time to sharpen the axe, but it's time well spent. We'll soon discover that we're actually able to accomplish much more in less time with a sharp axe.

Avoid Time-wasters

We need to regularly evaluate everything we do and to search for those activities that waste valuable time. One of the greatest time-wasters for many people, including bivocational ministers, is meetings. Church groups sometimes have meetings for no purpose other than that they are supposed to meet. Pastors are often expected to attend these meetings even though they have little to contribute to them.

Unnecessary meetings waste not only the pastor's time but also the time of the other attendees. Thus, churches should set some guidelines for meetings. The following may be helpful.

- Don't have a meeting unless it is absolutely necessary.
- Invite only those people who need to be there.
- Prepare an agenda, and stick to it.
- Set a time limit for the meeting.
- Begin on time. Don't punish the people present by waiting on late arrivals.

- Quit when the meeting is over.

Another time waster is procrastination. J. Oswald Sanders wrote, "Procrastination, the thief of time, is one of the devil's most potent weapons in defrauding man of his eternal heritage. It is a habit that is absolutely fatal to effective leadership."[10]

I find it is easiest to procrastinate when I don't want to make a difficult decision. Although the right decision may be obvious, I decide to make it tomorrow or next week. I may even spiritualize my procrastination by deciding to pray about it a little longer.

Please understand that I don't mean to minimize prayer. There are times when additional prayer is necessary, but there's also a time when prayer needs to cease and action be taken.

When we procrastinate rather than make a difficult decision, we're not only poor leaders but also time-wasters. We waste time by continuing to think about a single situation. It's far better to make a decision and move on to other activities rather than to remain locked in to one issue. We also waste time by losing the benefits that would result from a decision.

A bivocational friend of mine pastored a church that had a youth minister on staff. The youth minister was a college student who was expected to work with the youth on Sundays, with an occasional Saturday or midweek event included. Unfortunately, it soon became clear that the youth minister was ineffective. Coaching this individual did not help. My friend knew he needed to replace the youth minister but did not want to make that decision.

The youth program continued to suffer, and some youth stopped participating. The youth minister began to make excuses why he could not be at church on various Sundays. Finally, the situation became so critical that the pastor had no choice but to ask for the youth minister's resignation.

My friend wasted a great deal of time thinking about this situation even though it was apparent what needed to happen. Rather than seeing young people drop out of the youth program, the program might have benefited by bringing in a new youth minister sooner. Much was lost because my friend procrastinated. This is why Zig Ziglar tells people, "If you've got to swallow a frog, you don't want to look at that sucker too long!"[11]

Another time-waster is doing things that add no value to the church or your ministry. It's not uncommon for bivocational churches to still be doing some things they did in the 1950s but that long ago ceased being beneficial. "Many organizations, publications, or activities should never have begun in the first place. But they continue because people have grown accustomed to them, derive part of their identity from them, and would feel guilt-stricken if they let them die."[12]

A pastor told me his church once had two treasurers. One took care of all the finances; the other was responsible for sending in the mission money the church collected for their denomination. The pastor asked the mission's treasurer how she got the money to send to the denominational office. She said she would get a check from the church treasurer for the mission money, and then she sent the check with the appropriate form to the mission's office. The pastor asked why the church treasurer didn't simply mail the check. Nobody had a good reason except that was the way the church always operated.

It would be a good exercise to examine everything we do and question why we do it. We should do the same thing with all the activities of our churches. If these activities are not truly meaningful or helpful in achieving the vision we believe God has given us, we need to seriously consider stopping or changing them.

Television is another time-waster for many people. Some would be shocked if they logged the hours they watched television each week.

"You get done what you spend time doing" is a fundamental principle in my life. If I spend six hours a day watching TV, that will be my major achievement each day. Those hours could have been spent with my family, visiting church members, reading, writing, listening to teaching tapes, preparing for an upcoming conference or meeting, or doing physical exercise. All these would help me achieve my goals for my life and ministry, but I decided to spend that time watching TV. When we do this day after day, as many do, it's no wonder we can't realize our dreams.

Travel can also be a time-waster if we don't plan properly. In our family business we do service work in communities 20 miles from our office. Before sending a technician to a service call in one of those communities, we check to see if we have other work that needs to be done there. It's much more efficient for our technicians to do several jobs in a distant community, because it cuts down on the number of trips.

If you plan to visit someone in a geographical area, are there other people you could also visit there? Are there persons enroute you could visit? Some hospitals make available to clergy the names of patients listed according to their religious preferences. I've gone to the hospital to visit one person, checked the list, and found I had additional persons in the hospital I did not know were there. That saved me from making extra trips to the hospital and allowed me to visit with these folks sooner.

Use your travel time to listen to teaching tapes or CDs. Books are available in these formats too. Many versions of the Bible are also available. These types of materials are a great benefit to someone who spends much time on the road.

Always keep a book in your car for downtime. Recently I had two meetings on the same day that were a distance apart. There was a time gap between those meetings of a few hours. Rather than waste that time, I read a book I carried with me for such occasions.

Time-savers

Today's technology provides us with a number of tools that, if used wisely, can help us be more efficient and effective. Please note that these tools are assets only if they're used wisely. If not, they can waste our time and cost us money.

A computer is a wonderful tool. It can serve as a word processor for letters, newsletters, posters, or anything else you need to print. The church mailing list can be stored on the computer to provide you with quick information about church members and allow you to quickly print out mailing labels. Excellent Bible study software is available to assist the minister in sermon preparation. Through computers we can enter the world of the Internet and find virtually any information we may need on any topic. We can send E-mails to friends and family located anywhere in the world.

Despite the many benefits a computer can provide, many people still don't use them. Usually it's because of fear. They don't know how to use a computer, and they feel threatened by it.

Community colleges, computer stores, and private companies offer basic computing classes that can teach anyone how to use a computer. Many of these are very affordable; some are even free. Once you learn the basics, you can learn how to use many different programs. The advantages of being able to use a computer far exceed the cost of owning one and learning how to use it.

Cell phones can be time-savers but can also be very expensive if not used wisely. I carry a cell phone, but it is for my convenience. Only a select number of people have the number. If someone needs to contact me in an emergency, he or she can go through one of these people. As a result, I seldom pay more than the standard monthly fee for my phone.

However, the advantages of having it are great. If I realize I may be late for an appointment, I can call and let the people know. If I have extra time, I can call someone and perhaps squeeze in another appointment. I can call my wife to let her know if I'm going to be late. As long as one controls the cost, owning a cell phone can help a person operate more efficiently.

Some people still refuse to leave messages on answering machines or voice mail. Playing phone tag wastes an enormous amount of time. Leave your message, and wait for the person to return your call. While waiting for the call, you can be doing other things.

Small churches often don't have common office equipment such as photocopiers and fax machines. These can save the bivocational minister so much time that you should consider investing in them yourself if the church won't purchase them. For several years I had to go to an office supply shop to have copies made. This was very time-consuming, especially if I needed many copies. Once the church purchased a copier, I could make my copies and do other work at the same time.

Combination fax machines/copiers are convenient and inexpensive. However, if you need to make many copies at one time, these machines tend to be a little slow. The costs of fax machines and copiers are very reasonable. If possible, it's probably best to purchase them separately.

One of the simplest time-savers is the old-fashioned list. Spending 10 or 15 minutes a day listing the things you need to accomplish helps keep you focused on those things. You feel a sense of accomplishment when you check off a competed project, and you can move immediately to the next item.

Keeping the Sabbath

Remember the Sabbath day, to keep it holy. Six days you shall labor and do all your work, but the seventh day is the Sabbath of the LORD your God. In it you shall do no work. . . . For in six days the LORD made the heavens and the earth, the sea, and all that is in them, and rested the seventh day. Therefore the LORD blessed the Sabbath day and hallowed it (*Exod. 20:8-11*).

Many ministers preach more on this passage than practice it. Ministry demands so much time. Being bivocational adds the time demands of a second job. We can find ourselves working seven days a week before we know it. Many of us will try to justify it by saying, "We're just doing the Lord's work."

Ron Mehl was such a pastor. He consistently worked at the church seven days a week until he suffered a near-fatal heart attack. Read his powerful words:

But there are so many needs! So much hurt. So much opportunity. So many open doors. And somehow I keep wrestling with the idea that God "needs" more and more of me to get His work done. But the truth is, *I need more and more of Him.* As the church continues to grow, and the condition of families becomes more desperate, and the demands of the ministry go through the roof, I need more of His peace, more of His joy, more of His tenderness, more of His tough love, more of His wisdom, more of His resurrection life flowing through me. And the simple fact is He isn't going to give it to me in one-minute bursts between services or counseling appointments.

During my days of recuperation, I sensed the Lord saying to me, "Son, if you continue to run from Me on this matter, these things won't be over soon. There will be more breakdowns, because I didn't build you to work seven days a week. And by the way, *I didn't work seven days either!* If you think you can live your life without taking that time to let Me renew and restore you, you are mistaken—and I am not pleased! What I said to My disciples I say to you, 'Come with Me by yourself to a quiet place and get some rest.' "[13]

Until we come to grips with setting aside a Sabbath day to rest and reconnect with God, we will never be able to properly manage our time. We teach our congregations that the tithe belongs to the Lord, and we need to learn to live on the remaining 90 percent. Well, the Sabbath belongs to the Lord, and we need to learn to do our work on the remaining six days of the week.

Steve Bierly, a small-church pastor, cautions us, "We first need to recapture the idea of the Sabbath—spending one day a week totally away from our jobs. If you maintain that you simply can't do this, then you're setting yourself up as being wiser than God who commanded it."[14]

Some bivocational ministers have second jobs that make it easier to have a Sabbath day in their schedules, while others have jobs that make it very difficult. When I worked in a factory that required me to be at work five days a week, it was very hard for me to have a Sabbath day. In all honesty, I didn't have a Sabbath, and I paid the price in burnout and spending a year clinically depressed. During that time I was barely able to function and was of no real value to anyone.

As a business owner, I can now set my own schedule, and I take a day as a Sabbath day. During that day I rest and reconnect with God. There has never been one of these days when I did not fight the urge to do some work that needed to be done. The temptation is always there to make a few needed telephone calls or work through a stack of papers. I have to remind myself that my priority for this day is to rest and spend time with God. I am always more productive the remaining six days when I honor God by keeping the Sabbath.

Reflections

- What priorities have you set for your life and ministry?
- What system do you use to manage your schedule? If you don't have such a system, do you believe a system would help you better control your schedule?
- What personal growth plans do you have for this year? How do you plan to keep your axe sharp?
- List the time-wasters in your life. Which ones do you have some control over? What changes can you make to eliminate them?
- Do you have a Sabbath day in your life? If not, how can you start? How do you spend your Sabbath?

Notes

Introduction

1. Doran C. McCarty, *Meeting the Challenge of Bivocational Ministry* (Nashville: Seminary Extension, 1996), 28.

2. Linda Lawson, "'Tentmaking' Ministers Predicted to Become Southern Baptist Norm," *Baptist Press*, August 11, 1999, 1.

Chapter 1

1. Ron Klassen and John Koessler, *No Little Places: The Untapped Potential of the Small-Town Church* (Grand Rapids: Baker Book House, 1996), 20-22.

2. Steve R. Bierly, *How to Thrive as a Small-Church Pastor* (Grand Rapids: Zondervan Publishing House, 1998), 163.

3. Robert H. Schuller, *Success Is Never Ending; Failure Is Never Final* (Nashville: Thomas Nelson Publishers, 1988), 17.

4. John C. Maxwell, *Developing the Leader Within You* (Nashville: Thomas Nelson, 1993), 148.

5. Charles Stanley, *Success God's Way* (Nashville: Thomas Nelson Publishers, 2000), 3.

6. Edward R. Dayton, *Succeeding in Business Without Losing Your Faith* (Grand Rapids: Baker Book House, 1992), 41.

7. Leith Anderson, *Leadership That Works* (Minneapolis: Bethany House Publishers, 1999), 72.

8. John C. Maxwell, *The Success Journey* (Nashville: Thomas Nelson Publishers, 1997), 14.

9. Leith Anderson, *A Church for the 21st Century* (Minneapolis: Bethany House Publishers, 1992), 98.

10. Stanley, *Success God's Way*, 7.

11. Maxwell, *The Success Journey*, 11.

12. Schuller, *Success Is Never Ending; Failure Is Never Final*, 14.

13. Rick Pitino, *Success Is a Choice* (New York: Broadway Books, 1997), 3.

14. Ibid., 51.

15. Zig Ziglar, *Over the Top* (Nashville: Thomas Nelson Publishers, 1994), 28.

Chapter 2

1. Douglas G. Scott, "A Guide to Candidating," in *When It's Time to Move*, ed. Paul D. Robbins, vol. 4 of *The Leadership Library* (Waco, Tex.: Word Books, 1985), 43-49.

Chapter 3

1. George Barna, ed., *Leaders on Leadership* (Ventura, Calif.: Regal Books, 1997), 47.

2. Robert D. Dale, *Keeping the Dream Alive* (Nashville: Broadman Press, 1988), 13.

3. Andy Stanley, *Visioneering* (Sisters, Oreg.: Multnomah Publishers, 1999), 41.

4. Max DePree, "Visionary Jazz," *Leadership*, summer 1994, 18.

5. Stanley, *Visioneering*, 32.

6. Dale, *Keeping the Dream Alive*, 15.

7. Klassen and Koessler, *No Little Places*, 60.

8. George Barna, *Today's Pastors* (Ventura, Calif.: Regal Books, 1993), 36-37.

9. Rick Warren, *The Purpose-Driven Church* (Grand Rapids: Zondervan Publishing House, 1995), 81.

10. John Koessler, "Investing in Small-Church Futures," *Leadership*, summer 1994, 28.

11. Maxwell, *Developing the Leader Within You*, 146.

12. Barna, *Leaders on Leadership*, 53.

13. Warren, *The Purpose-Driven Church*, 111.

14. Ibid., 290.

15. Ziglar, *Over the Top*, 183.

16. Zig Ziglar, *Zig Ziglar's Little Instruction Book* (Tulsa, Okla.: Honor Books, 1997), 31.

17. Henry Blackaby and Richard Blackaby, *Spiritual Leadership* (Nashville: Broadman & Holman Publishers, 2001), 38.

18. Erwin Raphael McManus, *An Unstoppable Force* (Loveland, Colo.: Group Publishers, 2001), 193.

19. Blackaby and Blackaby, *Spiritual Leadership*, 64.

20. Barna, *Leaders on Leadership*, 50.

Chapter 4

1. Anderson, *Leadership That Works*, 62.

2. Ibid., 136.

3. Klassen and Koessler, *No Little Places*, 35.

4. George Barna, *Turn-Around Churches* (Ventura, Calif.: Regal Books, 1993), 50.

5. Maxwell, *Developing the Leader Within You*, 1.

6. Peter F. Drucker, "Your Leadership is Unique," *Leadership*, fall 1996, 55.

7. Franklin M. Segler, *A Theology of Church and Ministry* (Nashville: Broadman Press, 1960), 59.

8. McCarty, "Understanding the Bivocational Church," in *Meeting the Challenge of Bivocational Ministry*, 192-93.

9. Barna, *Turn-Around Churches*, 34.

10. Maxwell, *Developing the Leader Within You*, 49.

11. George Barna, "Nothing Is More Important Than Leadership," in *Leaders on Leadership*, 19.

12. Darius Salter, *What Really Matters in Ministry* (Grand Rapids: Baker Book House, 1990), 27.

13. Bruce P. Powers, *Christian Leadership* (Nashville: Broadman Press, 1979), 53.

14. Maxwell, *Developing the Leader Within You*, 58.

15. J. Oswald Sanders, *Spiritual Leadership* (Chicago: Moody Press, 1967), 53.

16. Stephen R. Covey, *Principle-Centered Leadership* (New York: Simon and Schuster, 1990), 124.

17. Sanders, *Spiritual Leadership*, 112.

18. McManus, *An Unstoppable Force*, 25.

19. Anderson, *A Church for the 21st Century*, 63-64.

20. Hans Finzel, "Creating the Right Leadership Culture," in Barna, *Leaders on Leadership*, 271.

21. Sanders, *Spiritual Leadership*, 70.

22. Segler, *A Theology of Church and Ministry*, 73.

23. John C. Maxwell, *The 21 Irrefutable Laws of Leadership* (Nashville: Thomas Nelson Publishers, 1998), 1.

24. Wallace Erickson, "Transition in Leadership," in Barna, *Leaders on Leadership*, 298.

25. Blackaby and Blackaby, *Spiritual Leadership*, 256.

Chapter 5

1. Maxwell, *The 21 Irrefutable Laws of Leadership*, 58.

2. Ibid.

3. John C. Maxwell and Jim Dornan, *Becoming a Person of Influence* (Nashville: Thomas Nelson Publishers, 1997), 20

4. John F. MacArthur Jr., *The Power of Integrity* (Wheaton, Ill.: Crossway, 1997), 125.

5. Charles R. Swindoll, *Rise and Shine* (Portland, Oreg.: Multnomah Press, 1989), 198.

6. "Traits of a Sexually Healthy Pastor," *Leadership*, summer 1995, 25.

7. Donna Schaper, "When Public Prayer Gets Too Personal," *Leadership*, winter 2000, 101-103.

8. MacArthur, *The Power of Integrity*, 132.

9. Jack W. Hayford, "The Character of a Leader," in Barna, *Leaders on Leadership*, 74.

10. David Wilkerson, "Our God Can Fix Anything," *Times Square Church Pulpit Series*, February 14, 2000, 2.

11. Hayford, "The Character of a Leader," 78.

12. Covey, *Principle-Centered Leadership*, 61.

13. MacArthur, *The Power of Integrity*, 83-84.

14. Swindoll, *Rise and Shine*, 202.

Chapter 6

1. Barna, *Today's Pastors*, 36.

2. Lyle E. Schaller, *The Small Church Is Different!* (Nashville: Abingdon Press, 1982), 71.

3. McCarty, "Understanding the Bivocational Church," 195.

4. Salter, *What Really Matters in Ministry*, 76.

5. H. B. London Jr. and Neil B. Wiseman, *The Heart of a Great Pastor* (Ventura, Calif.: Regal Books, 1994), 26.

6. Ibid., 37.

7. Blackaby and Blackaby, *Spiritual Leadership*, 110.

8. Klassen and Koessler, *No Little Places*, 40.

9. Ibid., 39.

10. London and Wiseman, *The Heart of a Great Pastor*, 20.

11. Georges Bernanos, *Diary of a Country Priest* (New York: Carroll and Graf Publishers, 1937), 28.

12. Barna, *Turn-Around Churches*, 46.

Chapter 7

1. Quoted in Salter, *What Really Matters in Ministry*, 43.

2. Peter Marshall, *Mr. Jones, Meet the Master* (New York: Fleming H. Revell Company, 1949), 32.

3. Dennis W. Bickers, *The Tentmaking Pastor* (Grand Rapids: Baker Book House, 2000), 73-89.

4. Richard A. Swenson, *Margin* (Colorado Springs: NavPress, 1992).

5. Brooks R. Faulkner, *Stress in the Life of the Minister* (Nashville: Convention Press, 1981), 21.

6. H. B. London Jr. and Neil B. Wiseman, *Your Pastor Is an Endangered Species* (Wheaton, Ill.: Victor Books, 1996), 185.

7. Andrew W. Blackwood, *Pastoral Work* (Grand Rapids: Baker Book House, 1971), 31.

Chapter 8

1. London and Wiseman, *The Heart of a Great Pastor*, 40.

2. Maxwell, *The 21 Irrefutable Laws of Leadership*, 165.

3. Warren, *The Purpose-Driven Church*, 394.

4. Anderson, *A Church for the 21st Century*, 238.

5. Barna, *Turn-Around Churches*, 69.

6. W. A. Criswell, *Criswell's Guidebook for Pastors* (Nashville: Broadman Press, 1980), 333.

7. Blackaby and Blackaby, *Spiritual Leadership*, 236-37.

8. Stanley, *Success God's Way*, 17.

9. Quoted in Warren W. Wiersbe, *Victorious Christians You Should Know* (Grand Rapids: Baker Book House, 1984), 14-15.

10. John W. Frye, *Jesus the Pastor* (Grand Rapids: Zondervan Publishing House, 2000), 56.

Chapter 9

1. Segler, *A Theology of Church and Ministry*, 115.

2. Maxwell, *The Success Journey*, 95.

3. Bierly, *How to Thrive as a Small-Church Pastor*, 111.

4. Maxwell, *The Success Journey*, 97.

5. Maxwell, *The 21 Irrefutable Laws of Leadership*, 43-47.

6. McCarty, "Understanding the Bivocational Church," 192.

7. Anderson, *A Church for the 21st Century*, 63.

8. Quoted in Maxwell, *The 21 Irrefutable Laws of Leadership*, 81.

9. Maxwell, *Developing the Leader Within You*, Introduction.

10. Rich Nathan, "The Price of Pastoral Leadership," *Leadership*, summer 1999, 32.

11. John A. Broadus, *On the Preparation and Delivery of Sermons* 4th ed., revised by Vernon L. Stanfield (San Francisco: Harper & Row, 1979), 7.

12. John MacArthur, *Rediscovering Pastoral Ministry* (Dallas: Word Publishing, 1995), 253.

13. Richard L. Weaver, *Understanding Interpersonal Communication*, 4th ed. (Glenview, Ill.: Scott, Foresman and Co., 1987), 24.

14. Keith Huttenlocker, *Conflict and Caring* (Newburgh, Ind.: Trinity Press, 1988), 38-45.

15. Ibid., 28.

16. Larry L. McSwain and William C. Treadwell Jr., *Conflict Ministry in the Church* (Nashville: Broadman, 1981), 38.

17. Charles H. Cosgrove and Dennis D. Hatfield, *Church Conflict* (Nashville: Abingdon Press, 1994), 42.

18. Huttenlocker, *Conflict and Caring*, 35-36.

19. Ibid., 23.

20. Ibid., 62-63.

21. Jim Yperen, "Conflict: The Refining Fire of Leadership," in *Leaders on Leadership*, 251.

22. Speed B. Leas, *Leadership and Conflict*, Creative Leadership Series, ed. Lyle E. Schaller (Nashville: Abingdon Press, 1982), 65.

23. Maxwell, *The Success Journey*, 99-107.

Chapter 10

1. Segler, *A Theology of Church and Ministry*, 75.

2. James Montgomery Boice, *Ephesians: An Expositional Commentary* (Grand Rapids: Zondervan Publishing House, 1988), 126.

3. John MacArthur Jr., *The MacArthur New Testament Commentary: Ephesians* (Chicago: Moody Press, 1986), 154-55.

4. Warren, *The Purpose-Driven Church*, 366.

5. Ibid., 367.

6. Robert Raines, *New Life in the Church* (New York: Harper & Row, 1961), 141.

7. Bob Russell and Rusty Russell, *When God Builds a Church* (West Monroe, La.: Howard Publishing, 2000), 176.

8. Ibid., 176.

9. Quoted in Maxwell, *Developing the Leader Within You*, 118.

10. Ibid., 126.

11. Swindoll, *Rise and Shine*, 116.

12. Maxwell and Dornan, *Becoming a Person of Influence*, 126.

13. Warren, *The Purpose-Driven Church*, 388.

Chapter 11

1. Henry Blackaby and Richard Blackaby, *The Man God Uses* (Nashville: Broadman & Holman, 1999), 201.

2. Herb Miller, "What Counts Most in Time Management?" *The Parish Paper*, December 2000, 1.

3. Maxwell, *Developing the Leader Within You*, 23.

4. Ibid., 27.

5. Ted W. Engstrom, *The Making of a Christian Leader* (Grand Rapids: Zondervan Publishing House, 1976), 101.

6. Hyrum W. Smith, *The 10 Natural Laws of Successful Time and Life Management* (New York: Warner Books, 1994), 101.

7. C. Jeff Woods, *Better Than Success: 8 Principles of Faithful Leadership* (Valley Forge, Pa.: Judson, 2001), 47.

8. Blackaby and Blackaby, *The Man God Uses*, 204.

9. E. Eugene Griessman, *Time Tactics of Very Successful People* (New York: McGraw-Hill, 1994), 150.

10. Sanders, *Spiritual Leadership*, 92.

11. Ziglar, *Over the Top*, 80.

12. Griessman, *Time Tactics of Very Successful People*, 87-88.

13. Ron Mehl, *The Ten(der) Commandments* (Sisters, Oreg.: Multnomah Press, 1998), 104-105.

14. Bierly, *How to Thrive as a Small Church Pastor*, 118.